T0334693

Cambridge Elements ☰

Elements in Perception
edited by
James T. Enns
The University of British Columbia

VISUAL–VESTIBULAR INTEGRATION IN CHALLENGING ENVIRONMENTS

Laurence R. Harris
York University

Michael Jenkin
York University

CAMBRIDGE
UNIVERSITY PRESS

CAMBRIDGE
UNIVERSITY PRESS

Shaftesbury Road, Cambridge CB2 8EA, United Kingdom

One Liberty Plaza, 20th Floor, New York, NY 10006, USA

477 Williamstown Road, Port Melbourne, VIC 3207, Australia

314–321, 3rd Floor, Plot 3, Splendor Forum, Jasola District Centre, New Delhi – 110025, India

103 Penang Road, #05–06/07, Visioncrest Commercial, Singapore 238467

Cambridge University Press is part of Cambridge University Press & Assessment, a department of the University of Cambridge.

We share the University's mission to contribute to society through the pursuit of education, learning and research at the highest international levels of excellence.

www.cambridge.org
Information on this title: www.cambridge.org/9781009518567

DOI: 10.1017/9781009518581

First published 2024

A catalogue record for this publication is available from the British Library

ISBN 978-1-009-51856-7 Hardback
ISBN 978-1-009-51855-0 Paperback
ISSN 2515-0502 (online)
ISSN 2515-0499 (print)

Cambridge University Press & Assessment has no responsibility for the persistence or accuracy of URLs for external or third-party internet websites referred to in this publication and does not guarantee that any content on such websites is, or will remain, accurate or appropriate.

Visual–Vestibular Integration in Challenging Environments

Elements in Perception

DOI: 10.1017/9781009518581
First published online: December 2024

Laurence R. Harris
York University

Michael Jenkin
York University

Author for correspondence: Laurence R. Harris, harris@yorku.ca

Abstract: This Element reviews the current state of what is known about the visual and vestibular contributions to our perception of self-motion and orientation with an emphasis on the central role that gravity plays in these perceptions. The Element then reviews the effects of impoverished challenging environments that do not provide full information that would normally contribute to these perceptions (such as driving a car or piloting an aircraft) and inconsistent challenging environments where expected information is absent, (such as the microgravity experienced on the International Space Station).

Keywords: vision, vestibular system, gravity, perceived orientation, self-motion, space, underwater

ISBNs: 9781009518567 (HB), 9781009518550 (PB), 9781009518581 (OC)
ISSNs: 2515-0502 (online), 2515-0499 (print)

Contents

1 Introduction

This Element considers the question of visual–vestibular integration in challenging environments. What is the benefit that might accrue from integrating the visual and vestibular systems in any environment? What do we mean by challenging environments? And why should we care how this integration may or may not be affected when we go into them?

We hypothesize that perceiving the world and our position in it requires us to build and maintain a representation of ourselves and the world as we move through it. Even if it were possible to regenerate such a representation afresh each time anything happens, it would be just too costly and inefficient: instead, we suggest that we create such an internal model but update it only as required. Others (e.g., Stoffregen et al. 2017) question the need to have an internal representation at all following the direction perception theorizing of JJ Gibson (1966) who suggests that all the necessary information is present in the stimulus without the need for internalization. An alternative approach is that some internal representation is required, at least for some select set of tasks. How is this representation constructed and how is any such internal representation updated as we move about our environment and change our orientation and position relative to the world?

Fortunately, the world provides a set of "common properties" whether or not they are used to construct an internal model. Gravity, for example, is constant and defines the down direction; light generally comes from above; our body is supported by our feet which are sensitive to the weight of our body pushing through them; and our muscles and joints are adjusted to support our body. These and other sources of information provide references within which it is possible to construct an internal representation of the direction of "up" and of our own orientation with respect to the environment.

The unfortunate reality for using sensory information to accomplish this is that our perceptual systems each have a limited functional range, take time to transduce the information with which they are presented, exhibit plasticity and learning, and tend to adapt to the conditions under which they operate. That is, the same set of external stimuli may produce very different sensory inflow at different times. Under normal circumstances, the process of cue integration – in which information from multiple cues is integrated – can help overcome such variations since the world is generally fairly consistent. But what happens in less predictable, "challenging" environments? For the purpose of this Element, we define challenging environments as those in which the normal consistency of sensory cues is not found. Such environments are particularly interesting scientifically because they help to illuminate the nature of the cue-integration and perceptual processes. Indeed, we often create such inconsistencies in the laboratory specifically to explore the mechanisms by which the senses are combined. But these inconsistencies are important when they occur in the real world because these *are* the challenging environments in which humans must sometimes operate. Being in a moving vehicle is an example of a challenging environment with which many of us are familiar. It is also an environment that it is extremely unlikely that evolution would be primed to address: there have been no evolutionary pressures for how to process actively moving at 80 kph while sitting down! In this environment, most of the visual cues (from inside of the vehicle) indicate no motion at all and the vestibular system, sensitive only to changes in velocity, indicate only the accelerations when the vehicle changes speed such as when it starts or stops or changes direction. The driver positions themselves so as to best obtain visual information about the movement of the vehicle and minimize conflicting cues from the inside of the vehicle, but the driver is still vulnerable to invalid information when, for example, a neighbouring vehicle close enough to fill a substantial part of the visual field, moves in some way unrelated to the motion of the driver's vehicle.

Cars and trains move in only two dimensions where orientation (the direction of up) is more or less constant. Aircraft pilots – fighter pilots in particular – must navigate in three dimensions where the limitations of the vestibular system signalling only changes in velocity become readily apparent. Although the direction of the force of gravity (equivalent to an acceleration) is signalled by the vestibular system, this signal is confounded by accelerations of the aircraft which can in certain circumstances be of sufficient magnitude relative to the acceleration of gravity to lead to the illusory perception of tilt. The insensitivity of the vestibular system to rotation at a constant angular velocity can also hide such a rotation in the absence of vision with disastrous consequences.

On Earth we are always subject to the force of gravity (except during free fall when the falling motion cancels the effects of gravity) which provides a constant downwards acceleration of approximately 9.8 m/s/s. Although variations caused by the gravitational pull of the Moon and Sun are sufficient to cause the tides, these variations are orders of magnitude below the forces to which our sensory systems are sensitive. On board an orbiting space station, however, one is permanently in free fall as the space station "falls" around the Earth. Here, astronauts need to function without the constant reference of gravity. The different levels of gravity found on other planets and on the Moon may also be consequential.

Before embarking on an investigation of the problem of multisensory integration in challenging environments, we should set some limits to our investigation. Here we will concentrate primarily on the integration of just two sensory cues: visual and vestibular, and two passive perceptual tasks: the perception of self-orientation and the perception of linear self-motion.

Let's start with what the vestibular system tells us. This ancient system embedded in the skull is sensitive to acceleration of the head – whether caused by active or passive movement or by gravity. It is therefore well positioned to inform us about the direction and magnitude of accelerations associated with self-motion (both linear and angular) as well as the direction and magnitude of gravity. This information is important for moving around the world and for staying upright while you do it. However, the acceleration information created by self-motion, even once disentangled from that due to gravity, is not in itself immediately useful. It tells you when you start and stop a movement, but this information needs to be integrated twice (in the mathematical sense) to produce a useful position signal that is needed to control muscles to keep the eyes and body stable through sophisticated reflexes. So, for movements that are maintained for any length of time, one needs to rely on additional sources of information. The most obvious source of such additional information is vision which although slow – the photochemical processes in the retina alone take around 70 ms (Wilson and Anstis 1969) – provides a rich description of the structure of the world and our movement within it.

There are many potential cues to orientation and self-motion, some of which are not instantly obvious. For example, humans can use olfactory information when navigating (Wu et al. 2020) and auditory cues can aid in balance (Teaford et al. 2023). Other cues include tactile cues (Harris et al. 2017b), somatosensory cues more broadly and proprioceptive cues. Disentangling these intertwined sensory signals is tricky. It can be impossible to stimulate specific perceptual systems in isolation. For example, the vestibular signal on Earth is always accompanied by somatosensory information from the support surface (except in the rather special case of neutral buoyancy – more on that in Section 6.2.1 and both the vestibular and visual system provide orientation and motion cues. The basic properties of our sensory systems have been well studied (see Frisby (2010) and Pokorny and Smith (2020) for reviews of human vision perception and Angelaki and Cullen (2008) for a review of human vestibular perception). The visual system transduces light entering the eyes but the complex photo-transduction reactions in the retina make it rather slow (Wilson and Anstis 1969). The vestibular system, on the other hand, being a mechanical system, transduces linear and angular accelerations within 5–15 ms (Liegeois-Chauvel et al. 1991). Whereas the vestibular system transduces three-dimensional linear and angular accelerations directly (see Section 2.1), the visual system must infer three-dimensional information about the world from the two-dimensional infor-mation on each retina. Whereas vestibular information is constantly processed and available, stopping you falling out of bed while asleep, for example, visual information requires the eyes to be open and actively directed around the world.

Our visual and vestibular systems have evolved in a three-dimensional world, within which we normally operate on a two-dimensional plane and our sensory and motor systems have evolved to meet these requirements. For example, the vestibular system is more sensitive to motion in a head-based coordinate system rather than in a gravity-based coordinate system corresponding to its involvement in head movements (MacNeilage et al. 2010) and there are comparable asymmetries in visual perception, for example, better acuity along the horizontal meridian than the vertical meridian (Barbot et al. 2021). This certainly complicates the problem of understanding how the perceptual systems integrate multiple cues.

1.1 Defining Self-orientation and Self-motion

Consider yourself at rest floating in a dark, three-dimensional environment in which there is no gravity: waking up on the International Space Station for example. Under such conditions, your perceptual systems provide no external frame from which to estimate the orientation or position of your body. Under such conditions the only possible definition of orientation is an egocentric one: using yourself as a reference with maybe your head as the origin and an arbitrary coordinate frame aligned with the long axis (to provide up and down) and the naso-occipital axis (to provide forwards and backwards) of your body. Let us now provide you with a visual world, still floating gravity-free but in a visually interesting environment. Now you have several choices for how you might define your self-orientation: either relative to yourself or relative to the now-visible world. Suppose you continue to define your orientation with reference to your own body, that is egocentrically. This must now be a constant with your head at the "top." Objects in the world can be assigned a position and orientation relative to your body but you can never move relative to this frame: the only movements possible in an egocentric frame are of objects in the external world. However, if instead you choose to define your orientation relative to an external reference, say relative to a particular point that you can see in the world, this now provides an "allocentric" reference frame relative to which you can move and change your orientation.

Now let us add gravity into the equation. Its direction can be defined relative to you (egocentrically) or relative to the world (allocentrically). Objects in the environment can define the direction of up (i.e., the direction of gravity) in many ways, such as by having an intrinsic orientation – a top and a bottom, like a tree – or by their relationship to each other – such as objects resting on top of a table (see Howard 1982). Of course, object-based cues to orientation can be unreliable – trees can fall over and objects can be glued to a tabletop.

Now, imagine that you are standing on a textureless, horizontal surface perpendicular to the direction of gravity (Figure 1a). You can now leverage the constant property of gravity to define your orientation. But the world is often more complex than this. Now, imagine that the surface plane is pitched up relative to your body (Figure 1b) – as if you are standing on a hillside. You now have a choice of several reference frames – you can choose to define the ground as horizontal (an allocentric decision) or you can use your body as the reference (an egocentric definition). Perceptually, neither your visual system nor your vestibular system will be that much use to you in this case. The vestibular system does not provide a very precise "up" direction: when disoriented in the dark at neutral buoyancy people make huge errors in determining the direction of up suggesting that vestibular information alone is unreliable (Brown 1961). And without visual texture, the tilt of the ground plane cannot be perceived visually (Beusmans 1998). However, your balance reflexes, using pressure information from your contact with the ground (Anastasopoulos et al. 1999) and your vestibulo-spinal system (Allum et al. 1995), can be relied upon to sense changes in your body's centre of gravity and activate your spinal reflexes to keep you upright. But perceptually, if you take the ground plane as your reference you are tilted, if you take gravity as your reference, you are upright. Does the ground rise to meet your feet in an egocentric frame, are you pitched backwards relative to a gravity-define one, or is your perceptual frame defined by some combination of the two?

Suppose we now add visual features to the inclined plane on which you are standing. The visually defined features; perhaps trees growing at an angle (Figure 1c, d) provide a third direction of up. In this situation, what frame

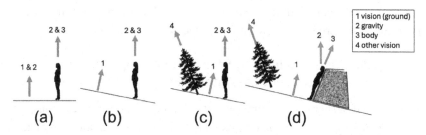

Figure 1 Some reference frames. The ground plane (a), gravity (b), the body (c) and other visual features (d), each provide different potential reference frames. Although these normally agree and are interchangeable, they can be quite different as suggested in (d).

might you choose to define the orientation of events in the world? One of the four possibilities shown in Figure 1 or some combination?

But now let us return you to the void but this time on the earth, and rather than being at rest you are undergoing motion. If this motion consists only of a constant linear velocity, then neither the visual nor the vestibular systems will provide you with any information about this motion. Now suppose instead that you are accelerated at a constant acceleration along the ground plane (still in the dark). You can perceive this acceleration (provided it is above about 0.05 m/s/s, the threshold for detecting such movements (Gianna et al. 1996)) but the signal created by your own movement needs to be disentangled from the acceleration due to gravity because applying two accelerations to a body is the same as adding a single acceleration in the direction of the resultant. Disentangling these cues is a complicated and inherently ambiguous task which has been the subject of considerable investigation and theorizing (Merfeld et al. 1999; Angelaki and Dickman 2003).

Now instead of linearly accelerating you in the dark we rotate you. The angular acceleration at the start and stop of the rotation is transduced by the semicircular canals and an appropriate perception of rotation is generated provided that constant velocity rotation is not maintained for more than a few seconds (Bertolini et al. 2011). Let us now bring you into the light and move you passively over a textured surface. Since you now receive both visual and vestibular cues to your motion you can generate a coherent estimate of your movement with visual cues making up for the inadequacies of the vestibular signal. This, even though the signals from neither the visual nor the vestibular systems are complete, nor are they necessarily consistent.

Fortunately, most of the time we exist in a world that is consistent. The lights are on, the ground plane is perpendicular to gravity or if tilted, there exist cues to this tilt (clouds in the sky, trees and other plants growing up aligned with gravity and so on). But there exists a wide range of environments that are not so "normal." We refer to these environments as "challenging" and provide a more formal description of this concept in the next section.

1.2 What Is a Challenging Environment? Impoverished vs Inconsistent Challenging Environments

As suggested Section 1.1, the arrangement of a given environment can conspire to make the problem of estimating self-orientation and self-motion very challenging. If you are put into an open cart in a rich visual environment and accelerated forwards, the visual system will be provided with rich cues about your movement and the vestibular system will capture any angular or visual acceleration. The processes responsible for integrating this information to provide a single estimate of what is happening will receive rich and consistent cues to motion. But not all environments are so forthcoming. Natural events such as snow or fog may reduce the visual cues to orientation and motion and consequently alter the visual perception of the speed of motion (Snowden et al. 1998). And, apart from when you are in an aircraft accelerating along the runway, physical linear accelerations are not usually maintained for more than a few seconds. Artificial visual environments, such as when watching a movie, may provide a challenging perceptual enviornment within which competing and inconsistent cues suggesting you are in a high-speed car chase while sitting on your sofa – yes, we consider this a challenging environment! The vestibular system is insensitive to constant velocity, and it is debatable as to whether the visual system is sensitive to accelerations (Mueller and Timney 2016): both systems have a range of operational limits and adaptation effects that complicate the reliability of any cue-integration or interpretation process.

1.2.1 Impoverished Challenging Environments

We can identify two broad classes of challenging environments. The first is one in which visual and vestibular cues are consistent with the real world but in which one or the other does not fully capture the underlying orientation or motion information (we refer to these as *impoverished challenging environments*). The vestibular system is insensitive to constant velocity for example – so driving a car at a steady 70 kph on the highway would be an impoverished challenging environment – and visual environments may provide useful cues in one dimension but not another. For example, an observer in an upright infinitely high cylindrical room that has been painted with vertical stripes such that they can perceive horizontal visual motion but not vertical motion.

The classic example of the challenge of an impoverished environment is the train illusion, reported as early as 1866 (Helmholtz 1866). The train illusion refers to the illusory motion of a passenger sitting on a stationary train looking out of the window. A nearby train that fills the passenger's visual field moves forward providing a strong visual cue that the passenger's train is moving backwards. The silent vestibular system may reduce the strength of this illusion but if the other train's movement is maintained for a few seconds, its silence is to be expected even if the passenger's train really was moving. The perceptual system's solution when presented with an ambiguous situation like this one often relies on prior experience – in this case that the passenger can expect their train to move – to select a solution (Berthoz et al. 1975). To solve this problem your brain makes a "best guess" at what may be happening.

Environments that combine visual environments that are lacking normal cues to orientation or motion, coupled with situations that are challenging to the vestibular system (i.e., lacking or experiencing only sub-threshold acceleration) can result in serious challenges for obtaining reliable estimates of self-orientation or self-motion.

1.2.2 Inconsistent Challenging Environments

A second class of challenging environments is one in which the cues available to the perceptual systems are inconsistent (we refer to these as *inconsistent challenging environments*). An example is an observer who is accelerating forwards while being presented with a visual display that simulates some other motion – for example: no motion. This situation occurs regularly in situations where the observer does not need to know about their movement relative to the outside world, such as a passenger in a plane or train or an astronaut in a rocket without access to windows. Sitting on your couch (no motion) which watching TV where the projected environment is rarely stationary, is another example.

Many video games – both virtual reality and screen-based – are examples of inconsistent challenging environments. The visual cues simulate – often very accurately – self-motion of the player but the corresponding vestibular cues – especially for prolonged accelerations – are lacking leading to sensory conflict.

In the microgravity of the International Space Station (so called because Earth's gravity is never exactly cancelled) nodding head movements that normally change one's orientation relative to gravity now produce no such sensory signal also leading to sensory conflict. And without the reference direction of gravity which is not well simulated by the visual environment inside current generation habitats, including the ISS, visual cues can be ambiguous. From the earliest days of space exploration, astronauts have reported a range of spatial orientation illusions (see Oman, 2003 for a review). Examples include the visual reorientation illusion (VRI), often triggered by seeing a colleague in a different orientation, in which astronauts suddenly feel that surfaces that were earlier perceived to be the floor suddenly become the ceiling, and vice-versa.

Scuba divers also commonly report spatial disorientation when diving either in poor visibility or even in very good visibility conditions but where there may be inconsistent visual cues to orientation such as being surrounded by a tilted underwater sandbank or within a submerged wreck. The resulting spatial disorientation can lead divers to fail to determine the direction to the surface, leading to situations that put the diver at risk.

The motion sickness that often accompanies especially inconsistent challenging environments makes this an important area of scientific investigation. To understand the consequences of such inconsistencies, environments with conflicting sensory cues are deliberately constructed in perception experiments to investigate the cue-integration process.

1.3 Principles of Multisensory Integration

The problem of predicting the output, given a set of input cues, has a long history in several different disciplines, from the integration of target bearings from multiple sources, to estimating one's position on a map or to combining multiple estimates of some property of a population. In perceptual sciences, investigating how inconsistent cues might generate a particular perception was established by Ernst and Banks (2002) who applied probabilistic modelling tools to demonstrate that multi-cue integration of visual and haptic information could be well modelled using statistical techniques.

There now exist several different mathematical models for obtaining optimal integration of multiple information sources. Each model makes its own assumptions about the properties of the input measurements and how one might choose to combine them. To place the problem in a general framework, suppose that we have a dataset D that we wish to explain with some set of parameters θ and we have some way of measuring $P(D|\theta)$. We have the problem of deciding how to choose the best parameters to explain the data.

1.3.1 Maximum Likelihood Estimation (MLE)

Maximum likelihood estimation (MLE) takes the frequentist view to choose the model that has the highest probability. To put this in the context of multi-cue integration, suppose that we have two independent estimates, each of which is corrupted by zero mean Gaussian noise. Then the optimal linear combination is the model that selects weights for the two estimates that are inversely proportional to the variance of the individual estimates. This model, which is now widely used in describing multisensory integration, makes strong assumptions about independence and the nature of the integration process between the two estimates.

1.3.2 Bayesian Estimation

One criticism of the MLE approach is the way in which the optimal values of the model are selected. The Bayesian estimation approach uses Bayesian cue combination to estimate the likelihood of values of some property S given different cues C. Bayes' rule provides:

$$P(S|C) = \frac{P(S) \times P(C|S)}{P(C)}, \tag{1}$$

where $P(S)$ is the prior distribution of S and $P(C)$ is the probability of the cue C. This is known as "The Evidence." Normally, $P(C)$ is obtained as

$$P(S|C) = \frac{P(S) \times P(C|S)}{\int P(C|S)P(S)ds}. \tag{2}$$

Note that this removes the explicit requirement to estimate $P(S)$ and ensures that $P(S|C)$ integrates to one.

The Bayesian estimation process is somewhat more general than the MLE approach described earlier in this section. With assumptions that are usually made, this generality can be lost, and in the limit with sufficient data the two models obtain the same results. These assumptions include that the Bayesian prior $P(S)$ is uniform, defined everywhere, and is positive.

As with the straightforward MLE approach, applying a Bayesian model to a given problem typically involves making strong assumptions about the nature of the probability distribution functions and their representation. Putting the problem in the context of multi-cue combination, it is common to assume that the individual cues are independent as well as conditionally independent. That is, for two cues A and B, $P(A, B) = P(A)P(B)$ and that for the property of interest that $P(A, B|S) = P(A|S)P(B|S)$. See Alais and Burr (2004) for details of an application of this type of approach to the integration of visual and auditory cues.

1.3.3 Causal Inference

The multi-cue-integration processes considered in Sections 1.3.1 and 1.3.2 assume that the question as to whether the cues correspond to the same real-world event has already been solved. This can be a trivial and reasonable assumption in a controlled experiment in the laboratory as the stimuli in question are presented simultaneously – although defining how close in time events occur to be simultaneous is an interesting question in and of itself (Stetson et al. 2006). Multisensory perception implicitly addresses the causal inference or binding problem. How do we know to associate the causal relationship between two events to integrate them? Perhaps the most straightforward mechanism for identifying causal integration is the use of some pre-defined windowing function that defines a fixed causality window. More recent approaches (see, e.g., Körding et al. 2007) model causality as part of a Bayesian multi-cue-integration process.

Within a chosen causal alignment process it seems reasonable to assume that vestibular and visual cues to a given motion or a given orientation always go together. But this is not necessarily the case either in experimental or real-life examples. So, for example, in the situation illustrated in Figure 1c, the two visual cues to orientation (the tree and the ground plane) and the person each give what would normally be regarded as reliable cues to orientation. Bayesian modelling would provide a single orientation based on each cue's reliability that did not match any of the contributing cues and would be wrong, misleading and hazardous to rely on. Instead, in this case, it might be best to disregard the tilted trees and rely on the vestibular cue. When the difference between multiple estimates is large, a person might exhibit robust integration in which the cue that is more discrepant is discounted or "vetoed" (Young et al. 1993; Landy et al. 1995; Ernst and Banks 2002; Rosas et al. 2005). Such robust integration can lead to changes in behaviour (Ernst and Banks 2002; Girshick and Banks 2009). In their review on causal inference, Shams and Beierholm (2010) discuss reports that animals that navigate using both path integration and landmarks give a larger weight to landmark cues if the two cues provide dissimilar estimates.

1.3.4 Data-Driven Models

Data-driven methods have revolutionized the process of modelling multi-cue integration, much like they have revolutionized approach to computation in a wide range of different fields, from financial modelling to machine intelligence. Rather than seeking to find a best "clean" model to combine multiple signals into a common output, one of a number of different neural network architectures are applied to the data problem and the actual process of modelling the computational structure is left up to the network to learn. Neural networks using various architectures have been proposed to both model the biological process of multi-cue integration and as a potential mechanism for machines to perform the same task (see Shaikh 2022; Xu et al. 2024 as examples). Such non-linear models can develop strong predictors for cue integration but inspecting them for the model that they represent can be complex. Weisswange et al. (2011) have demonstrated that a reinforcement-learning approach to multi-cue integration can learn a Bayesian-like multi-cue integration process and also demonstrate causal inference.

1.4 Where We Are and Open Questions

Perceptual cue integration is essential to a person operating in a realistic environment. Critical properties like self-orientation and self-motion perception are rarely recovered or recovered well from a single perceptual modality. The need for a multi-cue integration process becomes even more critical as the perceptual environment presents challenges to the cue integration process. In the limit, the agent may be presented with environments for which no unique reconstruction of critical world properties is possible, and the integration process may have to rely on environmental priors to obtain a consistent scene interpretation.

The perception of self-orientation (where am I) and self-motion (how have I moved) are fundamental problems. Even if no integration process is imagined, as argued in the global array model (see Stoffregen et al. 2017), the process of interpreting the complex and potentially inconsistent patterns that emerge may only be interpretable in terms of environmental priors. As the world is three-dimensional space, addressing these problems involves solutions in three rotational and three translational dimensions both for orientation and for self-motion. We consider each of these tasks in the following sections.

2 Self-motion Perception

Here we describe the perception of self-motion in a normal, well-lit, Earth environment. Most natural self-motion follows a complex path with continuously changing rotation and translation components. However, the study of self-motion perception typically investigates translational and rotational self-motion separately. There are many practical reasons for this decomposition, but one critical theoretical argument is that separate parts of the vestibular organ are sensitive to the rotational and linear acceleration components. Pure linear acceleration does not stimulate the semicircular canals while activating the otoliths, and a purely rotational acceleration does not activate the otoliths while stimulating the semicircular canals. Similarly, the types of visual motion that the two patterns of motion generate are quite distinct. So this behaviourally artificial but physiologically sound decomposition is appealing. The physical separation can never be quite complete; however, since there are two eyes and two vestibular apparatuses, the axis of any head rotation will almost always be slightly displaced from at least one otolith organ and at least one eye, and so even a "pure rotation" will evoke some centrifugal acceleration that could be picked up by the otoliths (Wetzig et al. 1990) and some slight translational visual movement as the eyes are translated around the axis of rotation.

2.1 The Vestibular Signal

The vestibular system is a bony labyrinth embedded in the skull which is continuous with the part of ear responsible for transducing sound waves. The organ on each side of the head consists of the three roughly orthogonal semicircular canals and two otolith (ear stone) organs, one arranged close to horizontal (the utricle) and other at 90° to this (the saccule). The horizontal canal and utricle are held approximately horizontal in most animals (De Beer 1947) but are tilted up in humans by about 30°, presumably connected to our upright stance. The vertical canals are not in the cartesian x, y, z planes but at 45° to this such that the posterior canal on one side is colinear with the anterior canal on the other. This arrangement allows them to operate in a push–pull fashion.

The semicircular canals have a limited dynamic range which is well matched to the dynamic range of head movements for a given species (Melvill Jones and Spells 1963). The otolith signal however is always potentially ambiguous, comprising components of applied acceleration and the constant acceleration of gravity. However, a comparison of the canal and otolith signals, together with an internally maintained idea of the direction of gravity, even in the absence of vision efficiently disambiguates this for frequencies above about 0.1 Hz (Merfeld et al. 1999; Green and Angelaki 2003). For lower frequencies, such as a maintained head tilt (0 Hz) or exposure to a maintained acceleration as may be experienced in an aircraft, tilt/translation confusions can occur, This includes the somatogravic illusion where ongoing translation can be perceived as tilt (Clément et al. 2001) and the oculogravic illusion where ongoing tilt can be misinterpreted as acceleration (Graybiel and Patterson 1955).

The response properties of the vestibular organs are complex but have been extensively modelled (Wilson and Melvill Jones 1979; Angelaki and Cullen 2008). The motion of the endolymph within the canals is sensed by hair-like cilia embedded in the cupula at the base of each canal (Figure 2). The

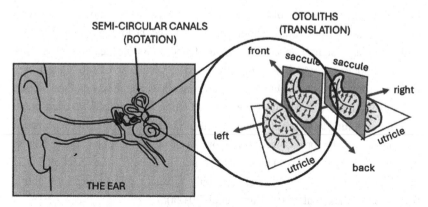

Figure 2 The Vestibular system of the inner ear showing the three orthogonal semicircular canals and the otoliths. The canals, otoliths and cochlea form an interconnected, fluid-filled bony labyrinth.

mechanical properties of the canals provide an effective integration such that the signal in the canal portion of the VIII nerve is proportional not to angular acceleration but to velocity over the range of normal head movements. However, although some responses are velocity-based, this still needs to be mathematically integrated to produce the position signal that is needed for controlling eye and skeletal muscles to make appropriate movement-resisting movements which led to a long and ultimately successful search for a neural integrator (Sylvestre et al. 2003).

The linear acceleration detecting part of the system comprises the otolith macula into which the cilia project. Each hair cell has a preferred direction of acceleration and provides the strongest response when bent in that direction. The hair cells are distributed over the two maculae (vertical and horizontal) in a systematic manner such that any direction of linear motion will cause maximum excitement for a unique set of cilia (Figure 2c).

In terms of self-motion, the vestibular end organ provides the brain with a signal that carries rotational velocity, divided into its components around three axes, and a signal about the direction and magnitude of the instantaneous linear acceleration (corresponding to which hair cells are most active). Central processes are then required to convert these signals into instantaneous position signals which are required for the eye and skeletal musculature to generate appropriate oculomotor and skeletal muscle compensatory responses and for updating our perception of where we are in the world and where we are heading.

2.2 The Visual Signal

Since the pioneering work of JJ Gibson, we have appreciated that vision provides important information about self-motion (Gibson 1950; Rogers 2021). Optic flow – the movement of features in the world relative to a moving observer – contains critical information about rotation of the head (comparable to the vestibular canal signal) and the direction of linear motion (heading) (Longuet-Higgins and Prazdny 1980) (comparable to the vestibular otolith signal) and, if scale information is available, the distance travelled and the speed of the motion (Redlick et al. 2001; Frenz and Lappe 2005). Optic flow on its own, even in the presence of a functioning vestibular system, can be sufficient to evoke a powerful illusion of self-motion known as vection. Vection can be either linear (linear vection – see Section 3.3.1) or circular (circular vection – see Section 3.3.2) (see Figure 3). Linear vection is especially effective for accelerations above 0.1 m/s/s (Redlick et al. 2001; Harris et al. 2012a).

Although accurate self-motion and heading perception is possible from optic flow when moving through a stationary environment – where all the visual motion

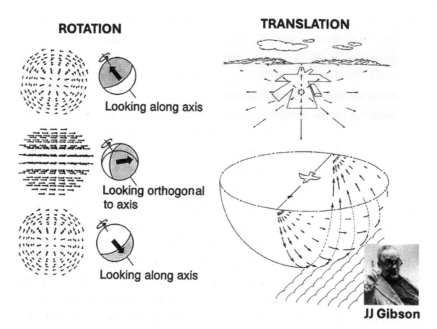

Figure 3 Optic flow refers to the motion of scene structure caused by the relative motion between objects in the scene and the eye. For a static scene, optic flow provides information about the direction and magnitude of self.

is generated by the physical motion through the environment – estimates of self-motion from vision alone can be disrupted by the presence of additional motion in the scene. Additional motion can be created externally by objects such as birds, people or cars moving within the visual field (Warren and Rushton 2008; Evans et al. 2020; Hülemeier and Lappe 2020) or even by the observer themselves by making eye movements that drag the retina over the scene (Warren and Hannon 1990; Warren et al. 1996). Such multiple sources of motion require "motion parsing" (Warren and Rushton 2007; Niehorster and Li 2017; Noel et al. 2023) to extract informative optic flow (due to the self-motion of the observer) from a scene that contains multiple sources of motion – as most natural scenes do.

2.3 The Complication of Eye Movements

The retinal movement created by movements of the eyes within the head may confound the problem of extracting and using optic flow, but they are a crucial part of the response to self-motion. In fact, in many ways, the perception of self-motion is the least important outcome of the combination of visual and vestibular information about self-motion. More significant are the unconscious responses: the compensatory eye and body movements that are generated to maintain clear vision and stable balance during the movement. One is not normally aware of the magnitude and direction of one's movements unless specifically asked to pay attention to them. When I get up from my chair and head to the door, I am not aware in detail of the rotations and translations involved in getting to my goal, merely that I am heading to the door. However, in a laboratory situation, I can be made aware of the components by being asked, for example, whether in some situation I have reached the door yet (see Section 2.7.3 for an expansion of this idea).

During self-motion the eyes are kept stable relative to the world by highly sophisticated compensatory three-dimensional eye movements known collectively as the vestibulo-ocular reflex (VOR). These are complemented after some delay by visually generated eye movements. The vestibularly generated eye movements comprise an extremely rapid and sophisticated set of three-dimensional reflex eye movements which rely on three-dimensional signals from the vestibular system to move the eyes to attempt to stabilize the image that falls onto the eyes in response to any and all motions of the head (Fetter et al. 1997). Although the VOR can compensate for rotatory movements of the head, thus nulling the visual movement and helpfully removing all the optic flow generated by head rotation, the geometry of the retinal motion generated by translation movements means that only the point fixated can be stabilized. The eye movements necessary to do this image stabilization then themselves generate retinal motion which adds to that generated by optic flow. This then is a problem that the brain must deal with to extract self-motion information from the retinal image.

2.4 Active versus Passive Movement

Perceptual processing of voluntary self-motion is potentially aided by having an expectation even before the motion begins of what is going to happen. This is true for eye movements – and is the main reason the world does not seem to swing around each time we move our eyes – and it also true for whole body movement. When initiating a movement, the brain creates an efference copy (Von Holst and Mittelstaedt 1950; Holst and Mittelstaedt 1971; Latash 2021) that is available even before the movement commences and can then be compared to the sensory feedback. This has the dual consequence that the world continues to appear stable despite being almost constantly in motion on the retina, and that we know where we are looking at any one moment (up, down, left, right). However, there are some imperfections in the system when taxed by modern faster-than-evolved-for motions and it is advisable to look where you are going when, for example, riding a bike (Wann and Swapp 2000; Hollands et al. 2002).

During active movement, in addition to the expectation and an efference copy of the motor signal, there is also information from proprioceptive sensors of the muscles, tendons and joints. Interestingly, the vestibular signals during active movements appear to be largely cancelled at the level of the vestibular nucleus both for linear (otoliths) (Carriot et al. 2013) and rotational (canal) (Roy and Cullen 2001) movements suggesting a reliance on non-vestibular and cognitive cues especially including efference copy during active movement (see Section 3.3). However, these experiments kept the head movements for active and passive walking the same – in real life active walking invokes a different pattern of head movement and therefore a different pattern of vestibular stimulation from passively riding in a cart: up/down and side to side components (referred to as "jitter") are introduced in addition to the overall translation. Adding eye point jitter to the visual stimulus enhances the magnitude of vection (Palmisano et al. 2011) and, in fact, any jitter seems to improve vection even if it is not associated with an active physical motion (Palmisano et al. 2014).

2.5 Egocentric and Allocentric Reference Frames

Questions concerning the perception of self-motion and self-orientation are tied to an understanding of the frame of reference related to these tasks. When considering self-motion and orientation we can identify two classes of reference frames: Earth-fixed (allocentric) and a body-fixed one. These were considered in Section 1 (see Figure 1). Although anatomically, the body is typically defined in terms of the sagittal, frontal and traverse planes (Figure 4), since many body parts can alter their orientation relative to others, it is necessary to be precise when referring to an egocentric frame. Similarly, for the allocentric frame, one could use the centre of a room as shown in Figure 4b but it would be perfectly valid to anchor the frame to any other point. As for the body, allocentric frames can also move relative to each other. It is impossible to move as a whole relative to yourself of course (as pointed out in Section 1.1) and so self-motion must, by definition, be coded and represented in an allocentric frame. This in turn implies an internal representation of the world in which one may move "in your head" with associated updating of the egocentrically defined positions of objects of interest (Blouin et al. 1998).

2.6 Self-motion: What Is Ground Truth?

It would seem straightforward to define what the "correct answer" is for how one has moved: it should correspond to the physical motion of the body relative

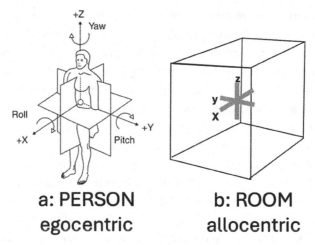

a: PERSON
egocentric

b: ROOM
allocentric

Figure 4 (a) An egocentric reference frame of the head and body for rotation (yaw, pitch and roll) and translation (sagittal, transverse and frontal). (b) An allocentric frame.

to some extremal reference frame. However, as observed above, there are an infinite number of reference frames to choose from. For example, if one were in a vehicle such as an aircraft, then the question of "how has the observer moved" will be answered differently for a pilot seated in their seat (who would answer relative to the outside world) or for a passenger walking around the cabin (who would answer relative to the cabin). Experimentally, we can manipulate separately the information presented to from visual and vestibular sources, for example by combining rich visual motion with minimal or no physical motion. An early example of such a deliberate presentation of conflicting visual and inertial motion is the work of Carpenter-Smith et al. (1995). Using the apparatus shown in Figure 5a, a prone observer was physically oscillated while presented with independently controlled visual stimuli. Figure 5b shows a system used by Harris et al. (2000) which provided physical acceleration cues (generated by throwing heavy weights over a pulley and down a stairwell) coupled with visual cues that can be driven by the physical motion (compatible cues) or controlled independently.

Figure 6 illustrates some technologies that have been used to provide conflicting visual and other cues while assessing the perception of self-motion. One interesting technical problem in investigating the perception of self-motion is measuring the physical motion provided to the observer. Researchers today can rely on accurate body and head tracking technologies. Mündermann et al. (2006) provides a review of the methods that have been used to capture the

(a)

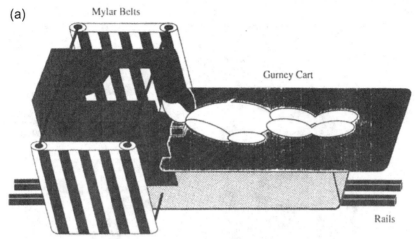

(b) **PRESENTING "VISUAL" TARGETS**

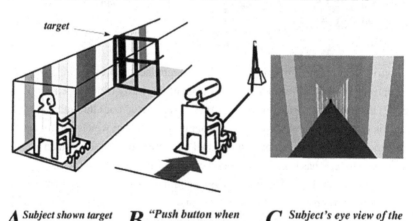

A *Subject shown target distance in helmet*   **B** *"Push button when you reach target"*   **C** *Subject's eye view of the virtual corridor.*

Figure 5 Apparatus for providing inconsistent visual and physical motion. (a) This part shows a sketch of an early approach that combines physical motion with visual motion induced by infinite visual rollers. (b) This part shows a sketch of a system that combines a visual display provided by a head mounted display coupled with physical motion provided by a weight system. Advances in virtual reality technology and physical motion platforms have expanded the set of experimental conditions that are possible. (a) This part is reproduced with kind permission from Springer Nature from Carpenter-Smith et al. (1995).

physical motion of an observer. However, how the observer actually moves and how they feel they have moved are often, especially in the laboratory, are not the same thing.

(a)   (b)

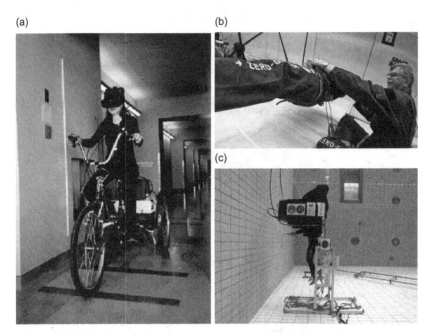

(c)

Figure 6 Sample environments that have been used to provide inconsistent or unusual cues to self-motion. (a) This is a virtual reality tricycle (Allison et al. 2002) that provides visual cues via an HMD and inertial cues through a tricycle. (b)This part shows an observer in a microgravity aircraft in which gravity cues to self-motion have been removed and visual cues are provided through an HMD. A similar strategy has been used to good effect during long-duration microgravity experiments on orbit. (c) This part shows a neutral buoyancy apparatus in which an HMD is used to provide visual cues to self-motion. (c) This part appears with the kind permission of N. Bury.

2.7 Measuring Perceived Self-motion

It would seem straightforward to record how much some combination of movement-inducing stimuli contributes to the perception of self-motion; however, the process is not quite as simple as it might first appear.

2.7.1 Qualitative

One complication is that vision-based perception of self-motion and vestibular-based perception of self-motion have different time courses and adaptation patterns over time. Visually induced vection, for example, is typically characterized by an onset delay and the magnitude of the motion perception may take some time to build up (Brandt et al. 1973). These properties can be used as indirect measures of vection or self-motion more generally (e.g., do you perceive self-motion yes or no? how long did it take you to perceive vection? what was the quality of the perceived self-motion? Judge the magnitude of vection on a scale of 1 to 100 relative to some reference condition and so on). This leads to measurements of occurrence or strength of the perception of self-motion (Kooijman et al. 2024) and is often sufficient when comparing the effectiveness of different conditions, for example.

2.7.2 Thresholds

The detection threshold (the minimum amount that can be reliably detected a certain percentage of the time) for detecting angular or linear self-motion can be assessed using rigorous psychophysical methods to overcome some of the confusion of earlier attempts that asked observers if they felt they were moving. A typical technique is to give two periods only one of which contained movement and ask the observer to make a forced choice looking for when performance reaches some pre-defined criteria. Using such psychometrically rigorous methods has shown some intriguing interactions with the testing paradigm (Pleshkov et al. 2022) – what you find depends on how you look – a certain level of quantum spookiness appears.

2.7.3 Distance Travelled

An important aspect of perception – assessing the everyday functionality of the self-motion system – is measuring how accurately an observer can tell how far they have travelled or rotated. Again, this depends on the question asked. If you (passively) move an observer and ask how far they have travelled for example by asking them to adjust a target to indicate that distance (Figure 7a) you obtain a different answer from if you show the observer a target and then ask them to

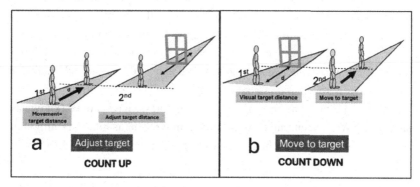

Figure 7 (a) Adjust target and (b) move to target tasks.

move through that distance (Figure 7b) (Lappe et al. 2007). Such techniques can be applied to visual simulations of linear or angular movement (Israël et al. 1993) or physical motion (Harris et al. 2000) (Figure 5b).

Of course, the results from such studies will depend, as we have emphasized extensively so far, on the motion profile, duration and transitions in the stimulus.

2.7.4 Choice of Stimulus

Psychophysically investigating the perception of movements involving the linear portion of the vestibular system is challenging because moving at a constant acceleration for any length of time results in high speeds and long distances of travel. Hence sinusoidal movement – with a constantly changing acceleration and velocity – has traditionally been preferred. Measuring the phase lag and amplitude of the response then allows comprehensive modelling. Even with the arrival of high-performance virtual reality technology, visual motion at constant acceleration results in similar limitations in terms of the difficulty of simulating very high-speed motion visually.

2.8 Summary

Self-motion perception is an intriguing aspect of perception involving the integration of multiple sensory cues to update our position within a representation of the world. How this information is utilized is the subject of the next section.

3 Mechanisms Underlying Self-motion Perception

3.1 Introduction

Our daily existence provides a compelling real-world demonstration that we can perceive our self-motion well enough to walk across the room, drive a car along a multilane highway and navigate through a crowd. Even walking across the room provides a rich set of sensory inputs. From the intent and command to move, the information from our gait and legs as we move, from weight transfer on our legs and joints as well as information from the visual and vestibular systems. Here we are interested in understanding how the visual and vestibular signals provide information about two aspects of our self-motion: the direction of motion (known as heading) and the amount we have moved (known as magnitude). We concentrate on translational movement as rotation – although often a part of navigation when it comes to going round corners – does not in itself get you anywhere.

Returning to the "moving across the room" problem, we begin by taking away the various inputs that are normally available to our observer as they complete this task and consider how performance is impacted. We then provide the observer with richer combinations of inputs and observe the results. We begin with the vestibular system.

3.2 Vestibular-Only

As the otolith organs provide information on the direction of linear acceleration, one would expect that our observer should be able to estimate heading when being moved passively in the dark. Telford et al. (1995) reported heading precision in the dark of around ±10°. Variations in heading direction can be both horizontal and vertical in either head or world coordinates. These can be separated by lying on one side when left and right in head coordinates become up and down in world coordinates. When lying on one's left side, gravity provides a pedestal for the now-vertical component of the left-right discrimination: meaning the discrimination is now between accelerations of $g + a$ and $g - a$ in the left/right plane instead of simply between $\pm a$. Using this manoeuvre, MacNeilage et al. (2010) found that heading precision or accuracy was surprisingly not affected by lying on one's side, confirming what they referred to as the "difference-vector" hypothesis, for both vestibular (in the dark) and visual heading judgements. They suggested this could be regarded as an adaptation to living under Earth-normal gravity and an independence of heading perception from the influence of gravity. See Section 6 for what happens in the microgravity experienced on the International Space Station.

So, given that a difference in sequential acceleration vectors can be discriminated with precision, can the brain perform the double integration of such an acceleration vector necessary to calculate distance travelled? The ultra-effective vestibulo-spinal reflexes provide an existence proof that this occurs, since the muscles require a signal proportional to their desired length – not their rate of change (or rate of rate of change of) length. But there is the question of calibration. Although theoretically the constant acceleration of gravity could itself provide a calibration, it seems likely that experience would be more reliable. Deriving position purely from acceleration can only be done effectively if the ongoing velocity and starting position are known. Harris et al. (2000) demonstrated that "distance travelled" can be obtained (from a stationary standing start) but that the gain (defined as output divided by input, or in this case, perceived distance divided by distance actually travelled) is not necessarily unity. In fact, when moving in the dark without other feedback, from an evolutionary perspective it is prudent to employ a high gain and err on the side of undershooting to avoid colliding with the target.

Experiments that rely on judging vestibular motion using visual targets run the risk of not knowing whether errors arise from the coding of the target or the motion. Harris et al. (2000) avoided this potential confound by presenting all the information physically. Observers seated on a wheeled cart on low-friction wheels were presented with a reference distance by being accelerated in the dark passively using a sophisticated system of weights and pulleys (Figure 8). The motion was then repeated, and the observer pressed a button to indicate when they had moved through the same distance. Accelerations were either fast (approx. 0.53 m/s/s) or slow (approx. 0.34 m/s/s) and target distances were repeated with different combinations of accelerations to avoid observers using the motion time to provide an answer.

The results and a sketch of the motion engine are given in Figure 8. Here the vertical axis is the true distance that the observer was moved when presented with a reference distance or the distance at which a visual target was presented, and the horizontal axis is the position the observer had reached when they indicated that they had moved that distance. The perceptual unity line indicates a correct response (gain of 1). Although performance is remarkably good over a large distance (8 m – the participant counterweight dropped down a multi-story stairwell to obtain this range), it is instructive to observe that a constant acceleration motion profile was chosen to provide an ideal signal for the otoliths.

A critical observation about the results described in this section is that they do not speak to the magnitude of the perceived motion associated with this physical motion. How far did the observer perceive that they had actually moved? As described in Section 2, there are many ways of asking an observer this question. Harris et al. (2000) accomplished this by having the observer view a visual target in the physical world. These data are also plotted in Figure 8b. Participants indicated that they had reached the visual target *early* relative to the physical motion that they had moved. That is, relative to a static visual cue, there is a significant over-estimation of the distance moved at constant acceleration.

The motion profile in Harris et al. (2000) was in the forward naso-occipital direction with upright subjects only. The question of the perception of the magnitude of physical self-motion in the inter-aural and head-vertical has hardly been investigated due perhaps to the difficulty of moving people significant distances at a known acceleration. Clément et al. (2020b) had supine observers pull themselves along on a rope in the vertical direction (relative to their body) while blind-folded. They found that travel distance moving upwards was overestimated (undershooting the target distance), meaning observers felt they moved further than they actually had as described in this section for forwards motion, whereas moving downwards was underestimated (overshooting

PRESENTING "VESTIBULAR" TARGETS

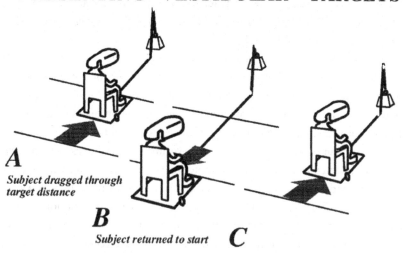

Subject dragged through target distance

A

B

Subject returned to start

C

"Push button when you reach target"

(a) Motion engine

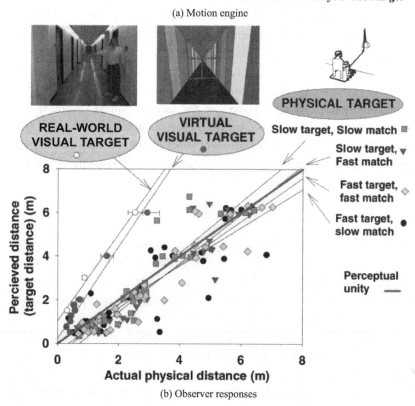

(b) Observer responses

Figure 8 Physical move to target. Physical-only motion data redrawn from Harris et al. (2000). Motion was either matched to a previously presented physical motion or to a virtual or real world visual target. (reprinted with kind permission from Springer Nature).

the target distance), meaning observers felt they moved less than they actually had. Clément et al. also performed these manoeuvres in a challenging microgravity environment but more of that in Section 6.

There have been efforts to explore the sensitivity of the vestibular system to physical motion in different directions while controlling for the direction of gravity. Bremova et al. (2016) identified motion thresholds for sinusoidal motion of an upright observer for gravity aligned motion and for motion in the plane perpendicular to gravity and showed thresholds along the vertical axis were higher than along the left/right and forward/backward axes, which they suggested reflected a reduced sensitivity to the predominantly vertical oscillations associated with walking. Kobel et al. (2021, 2024) provide reviews of the literature in their description of an experiment in which self-motion thresholds were measured as observers underwent linear, single-cycle sinusoidal motion either perpendicular to gravity or in the gravity direction, while either upright, supine or on their side. They found significantly higher thresholds for earth-vertical motion than for earth-horizontal motion. They also found a significant interaction between head and gravity coordinate frames, with head-vertical thresholds not being impacted by changes in the direction of gravity. However, the gain of distance-travelled perception cannot be deduced from variations in thresholds, and we await the outcome of further experiments.

In conclusion, physical movement in the dark (providing vestibular cues only) can be well matched to a previous movement but often shows a gain greater than unity relative to a real-world target meaning people tend to overestimate their movement in the dark – although interestingly this may not be true when accelerating downwards!

3.3 Visual-Only

The perception of visually induced self-motion either rotational (circular vection) or linearly (linear vection) has been studied much more extensively than for physical motion – partly because of the relative ease of generating the stimuli and because of the interest in virtual reality which largely relies on visual-only simulation. Vection has been studied since at least the late 1870s and is reported in Mach (1875) and Helmholtz (1866). The intention behind studying vection is to look at the visually evoked component of passive self-motion without the normal accompaniment of vestibular activity, generally taking advantage of the fact that the vestibular system is only sensitive to acceleration and therefore would not be active after the initial start of a constant velocity motion. These studies are typically instances of visual–vestibular conflict.

3.3.1 Linear Vection

Linear vection is produced by providing the observer with a visual stimulus that is consistent with linear motion. Classical stimuli involved loops of textured material stretched between rollers that were rotated so as to move the material past a stationary observer at a constant velocity. Much like the special effects found in movies of the 1940s, the fidelity of the visual stimuli was limited as was the ability to provide complex motion profiles. The arrangements made for the moving stimuli to cover different parts of the field were also limited. Modern computer graphics and XR technology has provided comprehensive flexibility in stimulus control, although generally still only in the central ±40° of the visual field.

There are many ways of measuring vection (see Section 2 and Kooijman et al. 2024 for details). Of particular interest here is measuring the magnitude of self-motion, that is, how far an observer perceives that they have moved. Before exploring this further it is important to recognize that any perception of vection will be highly dependent on the nature of the visual stimuli presented. No visual information is available when moving through a featureless void yet when sufficient visual texture is available the "train illusion" can be very compelling. This observation has led to a range of studies that have explore the importance of visual features in the scene and their location in the visual field (e.g., peripheral versus central) in generating useful vection (Telford and Frost 1993). One critical, but perhaps not unsurprising result is that for forward motion in the nasal-occipital direction, radial flow that encompasses the entire visual field, such as one might experience when moving along a tunnel or corridor, is particularly evocative (Harris et al. 2012a). Many studies have used this property as the default visual environment for exploration of the perception of self-motion from visual information.

Although estimating travel distance is essential to our ability to move through the world, our distance estimates can be inaccurate. Backward motion is associated with more overshooting than either forward, up or down motion (Bansal et al. 2024).

Recovering the distance that one has moved from optic flow requires infor-mation about scale. An expanding radial field of points could correspond to moving short distances at low speeds through a small pipe or huge distances at high speed through a remote field of stars. Although it was known previously that honeybees could estimate the distance that they had travelled from visual information alone (Srinivasan et al. 1997), Redlick et al. (2001) was the first to demonstrate that this was also true for humans. Utilizing state of the art VR technology of the day, observers were translated down a highly textured corridor and ask to indicate when they had reached the position of a previously presented visual target. The virtual corridor was modelled on a physical corridor at York University with which observers were familiar. The target was presented at different distances and the observer were translated under different motion profiles at either a constant velocity or constant acceleration (see Figure 9).

One particularly interesting aspect of the perception of linear self-motion is the nature of the motion profile used and the resulting visual display. A common assumption is that linear self-motion is smooth, as if one were gliding over a frozen surface. In normal day-to-day walking the pattern of footfalls introduces a cyclic vertical and horizontal shift in viewpoint of the observer which is

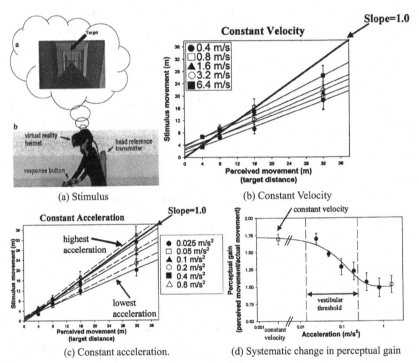

(a) Stimulus

(b) Constant Velocity

(c) Constant acceleration.

(d) Systematic change in perceptual gain

Figure 9 Visually induced self-motion to a target. For (b) and (c) the horizontal axis is the distance to the target in the visual simulation and the vertical axis is the distance in the simulation at which the observer indicated that they had reached the target. For constant velocity conditions the observer perceived that they had reached the target before they had travelled that simulated distance. For constant acceleration conditions, there is a systematic relationship between the simulated acceleration and response. (d) This part plots the perceptual gain (perceived movement/actual movement) illustrating this relationship. Redrawn from Redlick et al. (2001) and reproduced with kind permission of Elsevier.

not typically included in the simulated visual input. Supplementing visual optic flow with simulated viewpoint "jitter" has been shown to significantly decrease vection onset latencies, lengthen vection durations and strengthen vection ratings (Palmisano et al. 2000, 2011).

Much of the work on linear vection concentrates on motion in the forward, naso-occipital direction in a plane perpendicular to the direction of gravity. Given the wide range of asymmetries that are found in human visual information processing and the importance of gravity and other defined "up" directions in various visual tasks (see Sections 4 and 5, this Element), it is interesting to explore body orientation and simulated visual motion flow directions relative to the body. This space is only just now being explored systematically. Bansal et al. (2024) have shown, using the move-to-target paradigm described in Figures 7 and 8, that backward motion was associated with smaller gains than either forward, up or down motion. Harris et al. (2012a) used a similar protocol to Redlick et al. (2001) but had the viewer turn their head to the side and view the side wall of the virtual hallway (thus experiencing laminar flow that would normally be associated with translating laterally while looking straight ahead). Observers felt they had moved farther (higher gain) for a given simulated motion velocity (not acceleration as in Redlick et al. 2001) than for simulated forwards motion.

What of the potential interaction with the vestibular signal? During vection, the participant is normally not undergoing acceleration and even at stimulus onset the vestibular signal is silent. This conflict is accessible to the viewer who remains aware that they are sitting in the lab – although this conflict is responsible for making people feel "cybersick" during VR experiences (Teixeira et al. 2024). However, Jörges et al. (2024) found intriguing but an inconsistent interaction between the magnitude of forward self-motion perception and posture using constant acceleration forwards motion in which sitting was associated with higher gains than supine. This may be related to people's vulnerability to VRIs (McManus and Harris 2021) but suggests an interaction between vestibular cues and vection strength that was not found in heading (MacNeilage et al. 2010).

3.3.2 Circular Vection

Classically, circular vection is produced using a rotating drum, which for yaw rotations can be of quite small diameter as it needs only to enclose the head of the observer. The classical approach uses stripes aligned with the axis of rotation and when the drum is spun at a constant velocity around the head of the observer, they perceive that they are rotating in the opposite direction. For an upright observer this perception of self-rotation can take some time to build up and the perception of self-rotation can extend for some time after the visual rotation ends (Brandt et al. 1973). The sensation of motion is extremely compelling and unlike for linear vection, the observer cannot distinguish the sensation from physical rotation.

Inducing circular vection around the naso-occipital axis is also straightforward. A textured visual target sufficiently large to obscure any extraneous view is presented fronto-parallel to the observer and rotated. Inducing rotation around the inter-aural axis is more complex as the scene must be rotated around the entire body. One ingenious approach to addressing this task is to utilize a version of the haunted swing or illusion apparatus (Lake, 1893) (Figure 10). Here a large, full-scale environment is pitched around the observer. This device has seen many uses, both as the basis of amusement park rides as well as through the construction of rotating rooms for perceptual experiments, for example, Ian Howard's Rotating Room (Allison et al. 1999).

Many modern experiments eschew the classical "physical construction" of earlier experimental hardware and utilize virtual reality to provide stimuli for such experiments. This provides considerable simplification in terms of apparatus design and construction but introduces potential confounds related to the technology used to provide the simulated environment such as restrictions in the visual field size and depth distortions (Buck et al. 2018; Creem-Regehr et al. 2023).

As with motion transduced by the vestibular system, an interesting confound is the impact of gravity on the perception of self-motion. Wang et al. (2021b), for example, found that circular vection around the naso-occipital axis was weaker when the observer was upright, when vection was competing with the direction of up signalled by gravity, than when supine.

3.3.3 Other Sensory Contributions to Vection

In the real world it is impossible for physical motion to occur or for a posture to be adopted without stimulating more perceptual systems beyond just vision and vestibular. Since on Earth the body is always supported, there must always be a support surface where skin is being depressed by the weight of the body. This then provides somatosensory orientation information as well as information as to movement (Murovec et al. 2021). In Harris et al. (2017b) physical motion cues to self-motion were combined with tactile cues. Participants were oscillated in the horizontal plane in the dark with and without touching a stable earth-fixed surface. Providing tactile cues provided an enhanced performance relative to performance when vestibular cues were present. But it is not necessary to

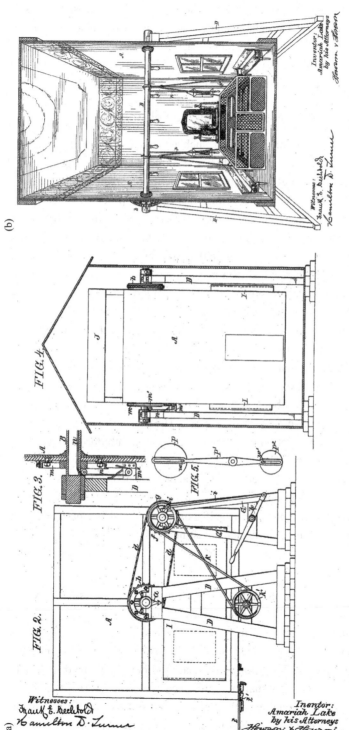

Figure 10 The Illusion Apparatus, also known as the Haunted Swing. Participants in a room remain stationary as it pitches around them. Reprinted from US Patent 508227A.

actually have physical contact with a hard surface to induce a sensation of self-motion. Seno et al. (2011) demonstrated that adding wind enhanced vection, and Murata et al. (2014) demonstrated that constant velocity wind provided a qualitative sense of self-motion even in the dark. Moving sounds can also produce or enhance vection (Murovec et al. 2021; Riecke et al. 2023).

3.4 Active versus Passive Self-motion

Most studies of self-motion perception, such as the ones discussed so far, have focussed on passive movement. Active self-motion, even ignoring the novel jitter evoked by walking, brings in the elements of prediction and agency (Rineau et al. 2023). Predictive coding has been proposed as a theoretical framework for multisensory integration for self-motion perception (Krala et al. 2019; Schmitt et al. 2022) but although we have important information about processing of active movement in the early stage of the vestibular system (Carriot et al. 2013), perceptual data are lacking. The apparent attenuation of neural activity during active movement raises a paradox (Laurens and Angelaki 2017): why ignore vestibular signals during voluntary movements at a time when they would seem to be most critical? Prediction and efference copy may be important here: the brain may predict in advance how each movement will affect the vestibular organs and compares the predictions with the signals it receives during the movement. Only mismatches between the two would then activate the brain's vestibular regions. This represents an important future direction for self-motion perception research. The passive vs active distinction corresponds to the perception vs action categorization introduced influentially by Goodale and Milner (1992, 2018) for visual processing, with separate pathways processing the different needs for action and perception, respectively. Here, passive movement corresponds to "perception only" (e.g., as when on a bus) whereas active movement is self-movement aimed at a particular goal and requires constant monitoring and adjustment (Merfeld et al. 2005a, 2005b).

3.5 Cue Integration

It can be extremely difficult, and sometimes impossible, to present individual cues to self-motion in isolation. Under normal motion in the real world, visual motion, vestibular motion and motion signalled by a range of other senses, provide coherent and consistent signals related to the observer's physical motion. For example, when sitting in a chair and being presented with optic flow to evoke vection, the visual motion is accompanied by a vestibular signal that there is no accompanying physical acceleration. How does the human perceptual system integrate such conflicting information? Averaging the two signals (moving and not moving) would produce a perception of movement with a reduced and ineffective gain.

Perhaps the most principled model of how visual and physical motion information is integrated under normal motion conditions is through a Bayesian cue-integration process. Such integration process is well reviewed in Angelaki et al. (2009). According to a Bayesian framework, cues should be weighted by the inverse of their variance. As a consequence, if the reliability of two cues were equal, then when multiple cues were present, the distribution of the combined signal would be narrower and the corresponding psychometric function steeper. However, if the reliability of cues is not equal, the resultant probability distribution of the combination of the cues would be shifted towards the more reliable cue. Such a Bayesian cue-integration model provides a compelling model for cue integration when the motion cues are identified as belonging to the same event (e.g., self-motion) and are consistent. But what if they do not and how can the perceptual system make the decision that they are, or are not consistent or are not associated with the same external event?

The "vision only" presentation of self-motion reported by Redlick et al. (2001) and reprinted in Figure 9(d) presents an interesting view into this problem. Here visual motion is presented at constant velocity and at a range of accelerations that span the reported range of the threshold for vestibular sensitivity to self-motion. The perceptual gain is plotted, with a transition in the perceptual gain from two different stages over this process. Within a Bayesian cue-integration process, one might explain this transition as one in which the visual signal weight remains constant over the range while the vestibular signal's uncertainty goes from "high" when the vestibular system is not receiving a signal indicating motion (acceleration) is present and goes to "low" when the vestibular system signals motion. This would explain the general trend from the two extremes but is less successful at explaining the magnitude of the combined signal at the two ends of the transition. Redlick et al. (2001)'s results suggest that the visual system provides a visual gain of approximately 1.75 on its own, but that when combined with a reliable vestibular signal, a perceptual gain of approximately 1.0 is obtained. In a Bayesian cue-integration model this would suggests that the vestibular system is operating well above threshold and producing a perceptual gain signal well below 1.0, the expected value.

One potential solution within a Bayesian framework is that the visual system "recognizes" that when operating in a condition of constant velocity motion, that it should artificially increase its reported perceptual gain as it is operating in conditions under which the vestibular system will not provide a reliable motion signal and then enhances the magnitude of its response to compensate. Such a model would violate the Bayesian model's assumption of combination of independent estimates of different measures of a common signal and instead resemble a causal inference model.

An interesting issue not addressed in either a capture or a Bayesian framework is the need for synchronization between the underlying signals. A surprisingly large temporal delay between the visual and vestibular signals can be accepted. Rodriguez and Crane (2021) found that visual and vestibular signals could still be integrated to estimate heading with a temporal delay of up to 1000 msec, between them but that this integration process began to degrade after a 500 msec of misalignment. This is considerably longer than the 100 msec delay temporal delay that is acceptable for head tracking lag in virtual reality (Allison et al. 2001).

3.6 Summary

The perception of self-motion is the result of a complex integration of information from multiple sensory and cognitive sources. Although stimulation of each sense separately (in as much as this possible) has revealed important information about each sense's contribution, how that information is put together suggests that the result is considerably more than the sum of its parts. Understanding this is an important goal for advancing our knowledge of how the brain works and has tremendous practical consequences for how humans can operate in challenging environments.

4 Self-orientation Perception

4.1 Introduction

The perception of upright is important because so much of our perception is predicated on the assumption that everything is the same way up: that is that it will be oriented in a consistent manner relative to gravity. The whole of the body's balance mechanism – involving almost every muscle in the body – uses this direction unconsciously as a reference to work against the force of gravity. Even your cardiovascular system requires this direction to function effectively (Negishi et al. 2017). At a more conscious level, knowledge of the "up" direction allows us to predict how objects will fall, and it provides a powerful prior for a range of other visual tasks which often depend on seeing objects and people the "right way up" for example when reading, recognizing faces and just interacting with objects and people in the world (Corballis et al. 1978; McMullen and Jolicoeur 1992; Rock et al. 1994). To obtain a glimpse into how important and subtle this prior can be, consider the Thatcher Illusion (Thompson 1980) illustrated in Figure 11. View this image from an upright orientation while the page is upright. Although there is something wrong with the image, there does not appear to be anything particularly wrong or unsettling.

(a) (b)

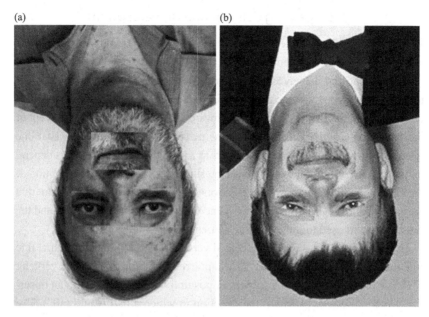

Figure 11 The Thatcher Illusion applied to the authors. View the image at different roll angles relative to the long axis of the body. At what angle does the image become "grotesque" rather than "natural"?

Rotate the page 180°. Now the faces appear grotesque. This is known as the Thatcher Illusion after the face image that was first used to illustrate the effect. This illusion depends on the angle of the image relative to the observer, and a range of self-demonstrations of this illusion and the angle at which faces transition from "pleasant" to "grotesque" can be easily demonstrated. The angle at which the perception of images of this kind transition is dependent on body orientation relative to gravity (Jenkin et al. 2004). Viewing the illusion at different body tilts is also informative (Stürzel and Spillmann 2000; Lobmaier and Mast 2007). Although this may be difficult if you are reading an electronic version of this Element, you can observe different "flip" orientations between pleasant and grotesque while maintaining your body at different orientations relative to gravity.

Determining the perceived direction of "up" is a complex, multisensory process involving integrating sensory information from many sources including the vestibular, visual, proprioceptive and somatosensory systems along with internal constructs and expectations. Our perceived orientation relative to gravity is critical not only for maintaining an upright posture but also to many aspects of perception (Rock and Heimer 1957): it specifies the relationship between our egocentric body-centred reference frame and all external reference frames.

4.2 Assessing Self-orientation Perception

When we are artificially held at some angle relative to gravity, such as when skiing down a hill, this unusual pose causes us to misperceive both our own orientation and the perceived orientation of other objects. Aubert in the nineteenth century noted that the crack in his curtains appeared tilted when he was lying down (Aubert 1861 reviewed in Howard 1982) which led to the concept of the *subjective visual vertical* in which the perceived orientation of a visual line relative to gravity shows systematic errors as a person is tilted. The errors depend on the amount of tilt of the observer, suggesting that it is in the misperception of the orientation of the body where the errors originate. However, it turns out that the amount and pattern of the errors depend on the method of assessment and the sensory system used to judge the line's orientation.

Three common measures of perceived vertical rely on lining up a visual line (the subjective visual vertical, SVV), a haptic rod (the subjective haptic vertical, SHV) or the whole body (the subjective postural vertical, SPV) with an observer's internal idea of gravity ("the direction in which a ball would fall"). The SVV is typically measured using the luminous line test which involves adjusting a line or rod to align with gravity. The SHV involves the observer manipulating a physical rod until the rod is aligned with the direction of up. This probe does not require vision and thus can be used without providing visual cues to orientation. One interesting variant of the SHV uses a tactile line drawn on the forehead by a robot (Beck et al. 2020).

Since the SVV and SHV tests specifically instruct observers to consciously consider gravity, they cannot be used effectively to assess perceived orientation in the absence of effective gravity, such as in the microgravity encountered in space or for brief periods during parabolic flight. Other tests that have been developed to remove this requirement include the shaded disc test in which the perceived concavity or convexity of a disc shaded from light to dark from one side to the other is assessed (Howard et al. 1990; Jenkin et al. 2004). This test is based on the assumption that light comes from above (Ramachandran 1988). Dyde et al. (2006) developed a measure of orientation that assesses the perceptual upright (PU), the orientation at which objects look most upright. This is known as the Oriented Character Recognition Test (OChaRT) and involves observers identifying characters whose identity depends on their perceived orientation (for example, the letter "p"). These tests are summarized in Figure 12.

For small roll or pitch tilts in the dark, the SVV is tilted away from true upright in the direction opposite to the body tilt (the E-effect) (Müller 1918; Betts and Curthoys 1998; Bortolami et al. 2006a) but for larger body tilts, the misperception is in the same direction as the tilt (the Aubert or A-effect, Aubert

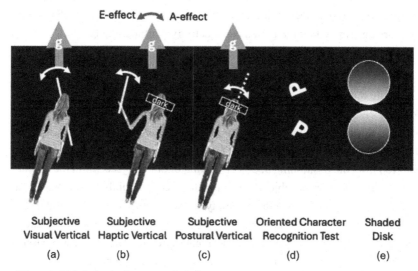

Figure 12 Methods for assessing the perceived vertical. (a) The subjective visual vertical (SVV), (b) the subjective haptic vertical (SHV), (c) the subjective postural vertical (SPV), (d) the oriented character recognition test (OChaRT) and (e) the shaded disc test. For the SVV, SHV and SPV methods, participants adjust or make judgements about the orientation of a line relative to their perception of gravity. If the line is tilted in the same direction as the body (relative to true upright), it is referred to as an A-effect; if it is tilted in the opposite direction, it is referred to as an E-effect. These directions are indicated above the SHV participant.

1861; Bringoux et al. 2004; Tarnutzer et al. 2009). The PU, also visual like the SVV, shows a larger and more consistent A-effect (Barnett-Cowan et al. 2013) than the SVV. The SHV shows a different pattern of errors again, with a consistent bias (larger than the SVV but smaller than the PU) away from the body tilt, an E-effect (Bauermeister et al. 1964; Bortolami et al. 2006a; Schuler et al. 2010). The SPV, the perceived orientation of the body, shows yet further dissociation from both the SVV and SHV (Mast and Jarchow 1996). In addition to these differences, interpreting perceived orientation using a visual stimulus is potentially further complicated by the ocular counter-roll reflex that rotates the eyes opposite to the head's roll. Indeed, the possibility that these eye movements are not adequately taken into account by the brain has been suggested as an explanation for the E-effect (Curthoys 1996). Interpreting the SHV is similarly complicated by potential errors in knowing the orientation of the hand holding the haptic device (Frith et al. 2000). Curiously, the subjective visual horizontal (SVH) is not at 90° to the SVV (Betts and Curthoys 1998) leading to the idea that the SVV may reflect otolith input (see Section 5.1) whereas the SVH may be more determined by integrated canal activity (Tribukait 2006).

4.3 Visual Cues to Self-orientation

There are multiple cues to orientation available to a static observer in a typical visual scene, comprehensively reviewed by the late Ian P. Howard (1982) and some of these are summarized in Figure 13. A visible ground plane and horizon are perhaps the most obvious cues, but orientation information can also be inferred from the positioning of objects resting of other objects, from the orientation of familiar oriented objects such as other people, buildings and trees, and from an assumption that light generally comes from "above" (Kleffner and Ramachandran 1992; Mamassian and Goutcher 2001). The light-from-above cue is the only one that appears to be innate (Hershberger 1970; Mamassian and Goutcher 2001) although this cue may not be as strong as is sometimes supposed (Morgenstern et al. 2011).

4.4 Non-visual Cues to Self-orientation

There exist several non-visual sources of information about the direction of gravity, including the vestibular and the somatosensory systems as described in Sections 1 and 2. The direction of gravity relative to the head is signalled by the saccule and utricle of the otolith division of the vestibular system in the inner ear (see Section 2.1). With the head in the usual upright position, the signal caused

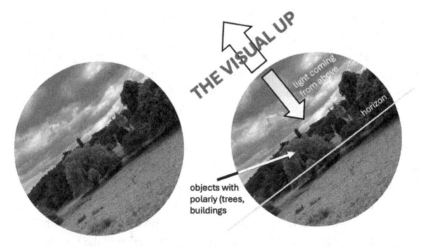

Figure 13 Visual cues to orientation. The image on the left includes many of the cues to orientation (indicated on the right image) from which the visual up can be deduced.

by the acceleration of gravity comes primarily from the otolith's saccule division which in an upright person is held roughly vertical (Fernandez and Goldberg 1976; Wilson and Melvill Jones 1979) (Figure 2c). During tilt, it is the ratio between the saccular and utricular signals that encodes the direction of gravity (Correia et al. 1968; Bortolami et al. 2006b). However, since, as Einstein told us, gravity is indistinguishable from any other linear acceleration (Einstein 1908), distinguishing the component due to gravity from the otolith signal during our normal movements around the world which also accelerate the head, requires some additional processing (Angelaki et al. 2001).

Any given head position has a history of how it got there – as its orientation changes through a sequence of previous positions. If this can be tracked, then the constant stimulation of gravity, once identified, can be disambiguated from other accelerations. Rotations of the head are signalled by the semicircular canal division of the vestibular apparatus and the canal signal is used by the cerebellum to keep track of the gravity component during head movements and to help disambiguate head orientation from translations (Angelaki and Dickman 2003; Angelaki and Yakusheva 2009). Thus, the vestibular system works as a whole to provide continuous updates to the internal representation of head orientation (Merfeld et al. 1999), even in the absence of vision. However, maintained head positions or slow movements below the threshold of the canals are not detectable (Angelaki et al. 2009), leading to confusion during maintained non-gravity accelerations, such as the oculogravic illusion (Graybiel 1952) in which tilt and acceleration are confused and an accelerating person can feel illusory tilt.

The direction of gravity relative to the body can be inferred from the vestibular apparatus in the head combined with a knowledge of the position of the head on the body, signalled by neck proprioceptors that indicate the state of the neck muscles and joints (Taylor 1992; Clemens et al. 2011; Fraser et al. 2015). But the direction of gravity relative to the body is also available directly from the somatosensory (touch) system that registers pressure on the skin where it touches a support surface (Anastasopoulos et al. 1999), and from specialized organs in the mesentery of the kidneys (Mittelstaedt 1996). Vestibular and somatosensory cues to upright can be partially dissociated by immersing a person in water at neutral buoyancy. The water then presses in with equal force from all directions around the body leaving only vestibular cues to orientation. This situation is considered in more detail in Section 6. A similar situation can arise clinically when somatosensory sensation is lost after neurological damage. Under such conditions a person can estimate themselves as vertical within about 5° but the A-effect is abolished when they are positioned on their side (Bisdorff et al. 1996; Anastasopoulos et al. 1997, 1999; Joassin et al. 2010). Patients with bilateral peripheral vestibular damage, who are forced to rely exclusively on somatosensory cues, show an abnormally large A-effect (Böhmer and Rickenmann 1995; Alberts et al. 2015), indicating that the errors in the SVV known from the nineteenth century may actually arise largely from the asymmetrical somatosensory and proprioceptive stimulation caused by adopting unusual body postures during testing procedures (McCarthy et al. 2021).

4.5 Summary

Building and maintaining a representation of our orientation relative to the relevant external frame, which might be sitting in a car, lying in bed, walking through a doorway, flying a plane, dancing or doing acrobatics, is essential for functioning in a three-dimensional world. Relevant information is transduced by several perceptual systems and combined to produce what seem to be multiple representations that can accessed separately by appropriate assessment tools. Are there then multiple simultaneous representations of self-orientation? And if one or many, how are they established and maintained and might they share a common mechanism? These questions are considered in the following section.

5 Mechanisms of Self-orientation Perception

5.1 Introduction

The observation that the perception of self-orientation depends on how it is measured suggests multiple, simultaneous mechanisms related to the different uses for which self-orientation is important. Brief introspection confirms this is true. We can read a book comfortably whether lying on one side or sitting upright where the letters all look "the right way up." At the same time, we are aware of the direction of a gravity-defined upright and of the orientation of our body, none of which may be aligned. If all the tests described in the last section accessed the same sense of orientation, then if the SVV were for example, displaced clockwise, the SPV should be displaced in the opposite direction by the same amount, but this is not the case (Mast and Jarchow 1996). How might these differences be resolved in terms of the mechanisms that determine them?

Clemens et al. (2011) suggested that there are multiple simultaneous estimates of gravity in multiple different references frames which are each tapped into differently by these various tests. When only the head is tilted (with the body upright), the SHV is accurate but biases in SVV are still found (Tarnutzer et al. 2009) which suggests that head tilt may drive SVV but not the SHV. SHV errors, in contrast, may be driven by the tilt of the torso and limbs (Bauermeister et al. 1964). Clemens et al. (2011) and Fraser et al. (2015) modelled gravity perception as having two distinct reference frames as illustrated in Figure 14,

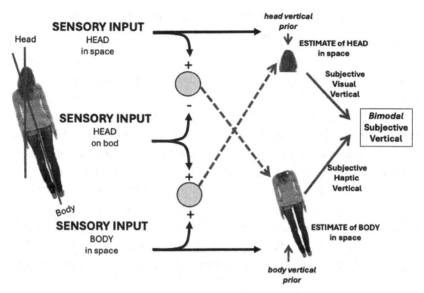

Figure 14 A model postulating two simultaneous position estimates of direction
of gravity, one based on the head's position (with indirect input from body-
based sensors, converted via neck proprioception into head-centric coordinates)
and the other based on the body (with indirect input from the head). In this
model, the SHV is derived from the body-based estimate and the SVV from the
head-based estimate. Figure redrawn from Fraser et al. (2015).

one inferring the position of the gravity vector using sensory information about
the head's position in space, the other using sensory information about the body
in space. Evidence for whether these are truly separate estimates comes from
combining haptic and visual cues to orientation using an illuminated but blurred
rod measuring the "bimodal spatial vertical" (Fraser et al. 2015). Blurring
reduces the reliability of the visual cue putting haptic and visual cues on a
more even playing field. Such bimodal measures show that the SVV and SHV
do not combine in a statistical optimally fashion. But when vibration is applied
to the dorsal neck muscles, thus disrupting the link between the head and body
representation of vertical, integration does become optimal (Fraser et al. 2015).
This suggests that the SVV and SHV access distinct underlying gravity percepts
based primarily on head and body position information respectively (Figure 14).
Differences between the errors recorded by the different tests can thus be
explained in terms of the different relative contributions of the head and body
to the judgements involved in each test. For example, the greater errors in the
PU (measured by the OChaRT test) during body tilt than found in the SVV can
be attributed to the greater contribution of the internal representation of the body
to the PU than to the SVV (54% vs 4%) (Dyde et al. 2006).

5.2 Somatosensory Information and the Perception of Self-orientation

Under normal Earth conditions, gravity is sensed by both the vestibular system as well as by joint weightings and muscle tension as the body is held in some orientation relative to gravity. Given the critical importance of being able to maintain a stable posture, one might expect a significant role of the somatosensory system in terms of maintaining an estimate of self-orientation. A key issue in exploring this relationship is the lack of observers with poor somatosensory systems but with intact vestibular systems to probe the role of somatosensory cues. The experimental observer in Yardley et al. (1990) suffered from a viral disease that left them with extremely limited sensation in their trunk. In experiments comparing this observer with normal observers, the experimental observer demonstrated no significant effect on the magnitude of the SVV when they were seated upright. When they were tilted 90°, however, a pronounced effect was observed.

Although it is difficult to obtain data from observers with non- or poorly functioning somatosensory systems, it is possible to disrupt or augment the somatosensory systems. Nakamura et al. (2020), for example, used a foam seat pad under the buttocks to reduce somatosensory cues for seated participants, and neutral buoyancy has been used to unweight the somatosensory system (Jenkin et al. 2023).

5.3 Perceived Self-orientation as a Multisensory Process: Bayesian Integration vs Causal Inference

All of the observations described so far indicate that self-orientation perception is a multisensory process with information arising from many sources that are used to update multiple internal representations of orientation (Merfeld et al. 1999). How visual and non-visual cues to orientation are combined is another example of multisensory integration (Mittelstaedt 1983). Bayesian theory suggests that the unbiased signals should be averaged, with each signal being weighted by an amount inversely proportional to its reliability (MacNeilage et al. 2007), together with the prior assumption that upright is aligned with the body – derived from Mittelstaedt's idiotropic vector (Dyde et al. 2006; MacNeilage et al. 2007; Clemens et al. 2011) and based on the expectation that we are normally upright. Provided that the reliability of each source can be quickly determined, this system provides a flexible "best guess" to the direction of upright. In this context, the A-effect is seen as arising from a system that normally improves precision during small head and body tilts but that becomes misleading during larger tilts because of the discrepancy between the contributing factors (Mittelstaedt 1999). When one source of information becomes unreliable, for example vestibular information during space flight, information from other sources would then be automatically up-weighted (Carriot et al. 2015) (see Section 6).

Causal inference adds another layer to such internal modelling by adding a "plausibility" aspect such that a sense that gives too unlikely an estimate is down-weighted independent of its reliability (Shams and Beierholm 2010; de Winkel et al. 2018a). Since there is only one "cause" being estimated – self-orientation – it is just a matter of down-weighting cues that don't agree with others (such as the body upright prior when lying down). This does not necessarily require high-level estimates of causality but can be achieved by the principle of robustness (choosing the most likely source) when one cue is not aligned with the others (Knill 2007).

5.4 Self-orientation and Cognition

Determining Earth vertical is not purely a consequence of context-free multisensory integration but can also be influenced by cognitive factors that depend on the demands of the task. We saw in Section 3 how active motion generates predictions about future states which can then be compared with the outcome of self-motion. Similar processes are involved in the perception of orientation as we described for self-motion. We constantly interact with the world and this interaction is a major factor in our ability to use orientation information to maintain posture and balance (Stoffregen and Riccio 1988). Our position is that we believe there is an internal representation of our body and its orientation which is updated in response to sensory information but is also affected by cognitive factors and available to conscious awareness. When standing on a narrow beam, SVV performance becomes considerably more precise (Bray et al. 2004) indicating that SVV is subject to alertness and attention. Awareness of being tilted (Barra et al. 2012) and mental imagery (Mertz and Lepecq 1998; Mast et al. 1999) can also alter performance on such tasks. The involvement of the temporal parietal junction (TPJ) in both orientation and bodily self-awareness (Tsakiris et al. 2008; Tsakiris 2010) may underlie these similarities between self-orientation and self-motion perception.

5.5 Summary

Figure 15 summarizes the principles of how we think the self-orientation system works. It is based around an internal representation of the body that is updated by the brain's estimate of the body's current orientation obtained by integrating incoming sensory information and also "cognitive attitudes" which include a prediction element about what is likely to happen in the immediate future.

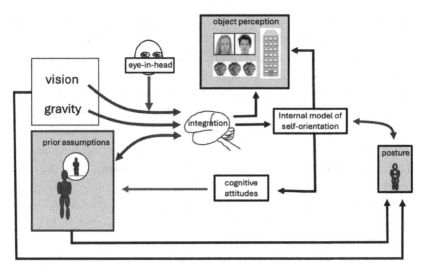

Figure 15 A summary of how the internal model of self-orientation is constructed and how it influences the perception of objects, our posture, and our cognitive attitudes.

Central to this model is that it is based around the fact that we are born, develop, live and die on the surface of a planet that subjects us and everything else we interact with to a constant acceleration of AROUND 9.8 m/s/s. Our sensory systems work within this framework and makes certain assumptions about how things are and how they should be. But this familiar framework is not always available. As our technology continues to develop, we find ourselves, more and more, in environments that challenge our perceptions and our internal model.

6 Visual–Vestibular Interactions in Challenging Environments

6.1 Introduction

The process of integrating visual, vestibular and other sensory cues to produce an ongoing estimate of self-orientation and self-motion has evolved to deal with the normal environment in which humans evolved and moved around on the surface of the Earth largely under their own power. What is remarkable is that with very little sensory enhancement, we are able to drive cars and aircraft, and function in a range of physical environments under very different visual conditions. How are visual and vestibular interactions affected by such environments? Here we review some of these environments, the impact they have on human performance and what this performance suggests in terms of multi-cue integration. We classified challenging environments as "impoverished" or "inconsistent" in the introduction and follow that distinction here.

6.2 Impoverished Challenging Environments

Perceptual environments associated with impoverished challenging environments are situations where sensory information is inadequate to do the tasks required. In these situations, the observer needs to bring their expectations and multiple cognitive aspects to bear to obtain an understanding of their environment and supplement the inadequate sensory information available.

6.2.1 Driving a Car

The visual information from optic flow while driving a car, truck or high-speed train will inform the driver about the direction of motion and a little about the speed. However, the normal oscillatory movements associated with normal bipedal locomotion are lost. For example, the viewpoint jitter associated with each foot fall are absent. Changes in the direction of the vehicle will stimulate the canals in the normal way, meaning that vestibular information is available but determining heading is a fundamentally visual task (Fajen and Warren 2000; Macuga et al. 2019) as proposed by Gibson (1950).

If driving is primarily a visual experience why then is driving in a car simulator so nauseogenic even when "driving" a training or research car body that is artificially mounted on a movable platform (Helland et al. 2016)? A major issue may be a lack of vestibular stimulation during the acceleration phases of the simulated car's movements. But in any case, by itself, optic flow is not sufficient for differentiating vehicle motion relative to the road and bodily motion relative to the vehicle (Chang et al. 2024). In this regard, even real car driving shares some features with travelling within a virtual world.

6.2.2 Flying an Aircraft

Spatial disorientation has been a contributing factor in aviation mishaps for decades (Previc and Ercoline 2004; Gibb et al. 2011) and pilot training now includes a significant introduction to the sensory issues involved (Naval Air Training Command 2002). The interplay between vision, proprioception and vestibular system is critical for perceived orientation (as described in Section 4) but pilots are vulnerable to errors in any and all of these sources of information. The infamous graveyard spiral is a potentially lethal example (Previc and Ercoline 2004). When flying in poor visibility, the exterior visual view does not provide a good cue to the aircraft's orientation. Such poor visibility occurs at night, in poor weather, and can even in good weather. When, for example, flying over water in the late afternoon/early evening pilots have few visual cues to their orientation as even the horizon may become difficult to discern due to haze.

Pilots flying without an instrument rating – flying under visual flight rules – are particularly at risk. If a pilot turns and banks the aircraft, their semicircular canals will at first transduce the angular acceleration but if the turn is maintained at a constant angular velocity for more than a few seconds the canals will be unresponsive, indicating to the pilot that the plane is no longer banking and thus suggesting that they should turn more aggressively. The resulting overcompensation has led to pilots that ignore their instruments – which have been designed, unlike the human sensory systems, to respond accurately in this situation – losing altitude and crashing. New technology such as head-mounted instrument displays may not help these problems and may even exasperate them (Rupert et al. 2016).

6.2.3 Sea Travel

Sea travel often profoundly challenges the control of orientation, and associated motion sickness is common. The associated motion sickness cannot be only the result of a sensory mismatch or conflict – for example the cabin remaining stable relative to you and thus conflicting with the pitching of the boat – since nearly everyone adapts to this environment, gets their "sea legs" and their seasickness subsides. An alternative, ecological theory involving recovering postural stability has been proposed that contrasts with the conventional sensory conflict approach (Riccio and Stoffregen 1991). A visible horizon when at sea both stabilizes the body (Mayo et al. 2011) and is related to postural precursors of seasickness (Stoffregen et al. 2013).

6.2.4 Perception in Low Visibility

Not all driving or boat journeys take place in perfect weather. Snow, rain, and other environmental conditions can confound and confuse a driver. Blowing snow and similar reductions in visibility shorten the perceived time to contact (Landwehr et al. 2013; Hecht et al. 2021) but alters drivers' perceived speed, making them think they are going slower than they are (Snowden et al. 1998).

Figure 16 illustrates the problem of low visibility as encountered by divers operating in cold fresh water. As in a terrestrial snowfall, suspended material – here particulate matter – obscures whatever visual cues the environment might normally provide to orientation and distance while at the same time introducing misleading movement cues to the observer. The light gradient seen in Figure 16 can provide an important cue to orientation at shallower depths. The suspended material may move in a consistent manner driven by local water motion when it can evoke a compelling sensation of self-motion. Similarly, pilots landing in a snowstorm can perceive erroneous motion of the aircraft due to the motion of

Figure 16 Diver experiencing aquatic snow.

blowing snow which can lead to potentially catastrophic decisions during takeoff and landing (Rasmussen et al. 2000).

6.2.5 Moving in Virtual Environments

Many virtual environments require the observer to be tethered in some manner to a fixed position in space. This may be due to simple engineering constraints – the display technology may be mounted the observer and must be tethered for power and/or data, for example – or it may be due to limits of the tracking technology used to monitor the observer's head motions and interactions with the environment. One common mechanism for providing a simulated visual environment to the observer involves having the observer wear a head mounted display (HMD) that obscures the view of the real world and then uses the display mounted within the HMD to provide a visual simulation of a virtual environment which may be the basis of a game, a training simulation or an experiment. Although users may freely actively rotate their head to view different parts of the simulated environment, usually they cannot usually translate freely beyond a small working space. This is despite the fact that they may be moving extensively in the simulated world, driving a vehicle or running around the scene. Even assuming accurate scene rendition, this then produces a sensory conflict between the vestibular signals and the visual scene. These conflicts can take the form of orientation errors or, more commonly, self-motion errors. Such errors are highly nauseogenic and evoke what has come to be called cybersickness (Rebenitsch and Owen 2016).

(a) (b)

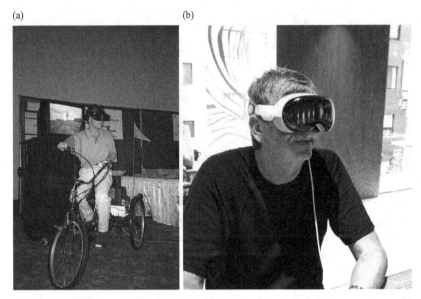

Figure 17 Aligning the virtual visual and physical worlds. (a) This part shows the VR trike. Trike motion is monitored by wheel and handlebar encoders enabling an individual to cycle around an extended visual world as head tracking is performed relative to the trike. (b) This part shows one of the authors wearing Apple's Vision Pro which can be worn while walking around a real environment.

There are some technologies that can overcome these limits, at least partially. Figure 17 shows two approaches to the problem. In Figures 6a and 17a, a standard tracking technology is mounted on an instrumented adult tricycle (Allison et al. 2002). Head motions are monitored relative to the trike which is itself instrumented. This enables physical motion within a large, simulated space. Figure 17b shows Apple's Vision Pro, an augmented reality headset which uses a tracking technology that enables the user to move about within a large physical environment. Note that it is critical to prevent the user from physically hurting themselves in the real world while they move about their simulated reality.

6.3 Inconsistent Challenging Environments

In inconsistent challenging environments, information no longer agrees with expectations. For example, when gravity is not present, the expectation that a head nod will change activity in the otoliths is no longer true and the reference direction of gravity is no longer present.

6.3.1 Long-Duration Bedrest

Many individuals, either due to age or physical impairment are restricted to bedrest. It has long been known that such immobility comes with it changes in physical condition that impairs physical performance (Convertino et al. 1997; Hargens and Vico 2016; Guedes et al. 2018). Many similar impairments are also found in space travellers, especially changes in bone, muscle and the cardiovascular system. Although merely lying down does not change any sensory input, after a while the internal representation may adjust to accept the posture as the new "upright." Given this, and the relatively inexpensive cost of such studies on Earth, long-duration bedrest has become a useful analog for studying the impact of microgravity on these and other biological systems. To maximize the similarity between fluid shifts found in microgravity and those found when supine, much of the controlled space-related experiments take place with 6° head down supine participants, as this minimizes the difference in fluid shift relative to that found in microgravity. Data collection takes place in specialized facilities that provide the necessary medical and experimental infrastructure to support individuals who remain in bed for long periods of time (see Figure 18).

The physical changes associated with long-duration bedrest also impact perceptual tasks. Perhaps the most widely studied of these relates to dizziness or vertigo. This impacts humans on Earth and is a well-known cause of post-surgical

(a)   (b)

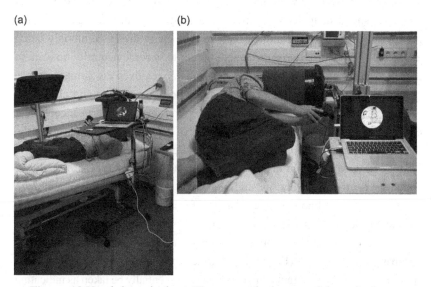

Figure 18 Head-down bedrest. Here a non-bedrest participant is shown demonstrating data collection in supine and left-side-down (LSD) body postures. Note the 6° head down tilt of the bed.

injury as otherwise healthy individuals experience vertigo as they attempt to move after post-surgery bedrest (Wang et al. 2021a; Mackenzie et al. 2024). Given the impact of long-duration bedrest on the vestibular system it becomes interesting to explore, for both terrestrial patients and for the safety of future space missions, the impact of long-duration bedrest on the perception of self-motion and self-orientation.

Long-duration bedrest (20 days or longer) reduces the effectiveness of visual cues in determining upright (Harris et al. 2022) which suggests that bedrest increases the reliance of egocentric cues (the assumption that up is aligned with the body) an effect that is also found during long-duration microgravity. This would seem to be paradoxical for a person lying horizontal but reflects the body's best guess about the ongoing situation.

Less is known about the impact of long-duration bedrest on the perception of self-motion and in vection. Bedrest does impact the speed of normal walking post-bed-rest (Grassi et al. 2024) but this is an indirect measure and confounded by the muscular and other impacts of bedrest.

In summary, after being forced to maintain a horizontal posture for several days, even in a normally oriented, visible room, people tend to revert to regarding their own bodies as their most reliable frame of reference.

6.3.2 Neutral Buoyancy

The neutral buoyant environment plagues both recreational and commercial divers. Suspended, underwater divers are buoyed by the increased specific gravity of the water environment relative to air with divers commonly being augmented with extra (dense) weights in order to become neutrally buoyant in their environment. Neutral buoyancy essentially removes the somatosensory system as a contributor to information about body orientation and allows the vestibular system to work unaided. Thus, it is an example of an inconsistent challenging environment in which one source of expected information about the direction of gravity is missing. From a visual point of view the use of Scuba goggles may magnify and distort the participant's view of their surroundings, which can itself provide unusual and even misleading cues of self-orientation in the environment. Although advertisements for recreational Scuba divers often present a clear and visually clear environment, suspended particulate matter in the water column, often referred to as aquatic snow, can obscure naturally occurring visual texture (Figure 16). Furthermore, driven by the current, this snow can move in a coherent manner which can potentially be taken as indicating an (incorrect) direction or motion.

Given the potentially perceptually confusing nature of the environment, as part of their training, divers are taught to utilize other cues to estimate their self-orientation. One common strategy, for example, is to utilize the direction of the motion of bubbles as a reliable cue the direction of up.

Neutral buoyancy has been used as an analog for the microgravity conditions found in space even before manned space travel (Trout 1967; Neufeld and Charles 2015). Figure 19 shows views of the neutral buoyancy facilities at ESA

(a)

(b)

Figure 19 Large-scale neutral buoyancy facilities associated with ESA (a) and NASA (b). These facilities are used for astronaut training and task rehearsal. Human performance experiments are typically performed in more general-purpose pool facilities.

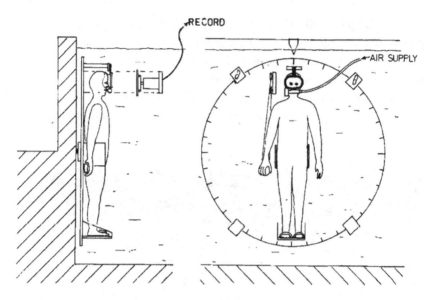

Figure 20 Measuring the subjective visual vertical and perceived body tilt at neutral buoyancy. Reprinted from Lechner-Steinleitner and Schone (1980) with kind permission from Springer Nature.

and at NASA. However, neutral buoyancy is not a perfect model for microgravity since divers and their tools are still exposed to gravity! But given its existence as a challenging environment for commercial and recreational activities on Earth, and its use as an analog environment for space travel, there have been several efforts to understand how the perception of self-orientation and self-motion are impacted by this unique environment.

Several studies that have explored the effect of water immersion on balance and the perception of self-orientation. For example, Glass et al. (2018) investigated the impact of long-term immersion on balance upon return to a non-buoyant environment, and others (Brown 1961; Wade 1973; Lechner-Steinleitner and Schone 1980) have compared the perception of self-orientation under neutral buoyancy conditions with responses under terrestrial conditions and found the expected reduction in accuracy. See Figure 20 for the sort of equipment used. Jenkin et al. (2023) utilized the OChaRT probe (see Section 4.2 and Figure 6c) to investigate the impact of neutral buoyancy on the perception of self-orientation and found that visual cues had a reduced effect in contributing to participant's direction of up. That being said, they found no significant change in the weightings of visual, body and gravity cues in terms of a linear vector sum model of the perceived direction of up.

Fewer experiments have quantified the effect of neutral buoyancy on the perception of self-motion. Fauville et al. (2021) conducted an active self-motion experiment which demonstrated a significantly larger estimate of their distance travelled when floating prone versus standing upright while experiencing motion in a VR simulation. However, Bury et al. (2023) found no significant difference in vection between in-lab (not neutrally buoyant) and in-pool (neutrally buoyant) conditions as measured through either self-reported vection or through the Move-to-Target or Adjust-Target tasks described in Section 2.7.3. Bury et al.'s work used a more controlled motion profile than that employed by Fauville et al. (2021), suggesting that although neutral buoyancy can impact the way in which visual cues are used to establish self-orientation, this is not the case for self-motion estimation.

6.3.3 Microgravity

Space is perhaps the most challenging environment in which humans have regularly placed themselves. Humans have been exposed to hours of continuous microgravity since the early 1960s and space habitats have provided multiple days of continuous microgravity since the Apollo missions of the late 1960s and early 1970s. The International Space Station (ISS) has been continuously inhabited since November 2, 2000. The station orbits at around 250 km from the Earth's surface but is in continuous freefall around the Earth, essentially but not precisely cancelling gravity by its motion: hence the reference to the remaining microgravity. The vast majority of space travellers to date are highly trained individuals, with higher-than-average performance over almost every measurable scale. (The current requirements for being accepted into the US Astronaut Corps requires, among, other requirements, either the completion of a master's degree in a STEM subject or 1000 pilot hours in a jet aircraft.) But this specialized sampling of humans is likely to change in the future, and it is likely that more and more untrained space tourists, and people selected for specific skills not normally associated with the international astronaut corps will be venturing into space in the coming years.

Being in a microgravity environment produces multiple issues for the human body, especially for the cardiovascular, muscle, bone and immune systems (Iwase et al. 2020) as well as potential damage to the eyes (Paez et al. 2020), liver (Vinken 2022) and brain (Burles et al. 2024) and affects perceived eye height (Bourrelly et al. 2015), time perception (Navarro Morales et al. 2023) and other aspects of cognitive functioning which are very important when speculating about very-long-term exposure to microgravity such as on a voyage to Mars. Almost 70 percent of astronauts experience motion sickness within the first 3 or 4 days of arriving in space (Lackner and Dizio 2006). Here we are concerned specifically about visual–vestibular interaction and how the unloading of the otolith system (Carriot et al. 2021) affects orientation and self-motion perception. Access to astronauts for perceptual experiments is quite limited but microgravity can also be achieved by flying in a parabolic trajectory to cancel gravity (see Figure 6b). Unfortunately, due to the restricted height of the atmosphere, such manoeuvres can only generate approximately 22s of microgravity at a time but this can be repeated multiple times providing a more accessible experimental time.

Orientation Perception in Microgravity

The perception of self-orientation during a space mission is critical for mission success and astronaut safety. For example, toggle switches have a polarity that is usually tied to a common understanding of up. Misperceiving whether a switch is on or off could be consequential. The Neurolab Space Mission in 1998 (STS 90) provided an early opportunity to explore the effect of microgravity on the perception of self-orientation. Although hampered by a small sample size, experiments on Neurolab (Buckey and Homick 2003) provided compelling new information about the relationship between microgravity and self-orientation. For example, Clément and colleagues sent a human centrifuge onboard Neurolab (Clément et al. 2001, 2003) with which they were able to demonstrate that the centripetal force created by a spinning centrifuge could create the sensation of tilt in microgravity. In one condition their participants sat on a chair mounted on the centrifuge such that their bodies were aligned with the axis of rotation but offset from it, with left ear in/right ear out. The centripetal force was therefore at 90° to the long axis of their body. Participants felt a strong somatogravic illusion, an illusionary perception of body tilt, which reached 83° towards the end of the 16-day mission when exposed to 1 G of centripetal force and about 48° during exposure to 0.5 G. This supported the model that the otolith system responded normally in space and that not only the direction but also the magnitude of a maintained acceleration was taken into account by the brain. Interestingly, the linear acceleration of the centripetal force never produced the sensation of translation contributing to the extensive debate about the otolith-tilt-translation-reinterpretation (OTTR) hypothesis (see Parker et al. 1985; Merfeld 2003 and Clark 2019 for detailed reviews).

Judging self-orientation becomes a rather different concept when in the microgravity of low-earth orbit or during parabolic flight, in which the effects of gravity are essentially cancelled by the movement of the vehicle. If an astronaut closes their eyes they lose all sense of spatial reference (Lackner and DiZio 2000). Logically, with eyes open, they could just pick a surface in the space craft and arbitrarily identify it as "the floor" to use as a consistent visual reference for their self-orientation (allocentric) or they could revert to the prior that "up" is always in the direction of their head (egocentric). Either of these choices would lead to rather unstable perceptions (not aided by the inconsistent architecture of the ISS). In early space missions (e.g., Gemini), astronauts remained in their seats throughout the mission. As mission duration increased however, astronauts began to perform tasks that required them to move about the cabin or to perform extra-vehicular activities (EVA's or spacewalks). As they did so, they reported orientation illusions including suddenly feeling upside down when another crew member entered the cabin in an inverted orientation: a VRIs in which their perceived orientation suddenly flipped (Lackner and DiZio 2000; Oman 2007). With the effective absence of gravity leaving only the body and vision as potential cues to upright, the weighting of the visual contribution is adjusted so as to maintain the relative contributions of vision and body found on Earth (Harris et al. 2017a). Young et al. (1984) used the rod and frame test to look at the influence of the environment (the frame). They found that astronauts employed a range of strategies but that those more dependent on the environment (as tested on Earth) became even more environmentally dependent after their flight but recovered by about six days after return to Earth. Harris et al. (2017a) demonstrated that astronauts become less dependent on visual cues in terms of their perception of the direction of up upon arriving in microgravity and that this change is maintained long after return to Earth.

If somatosensory cues to orientation are provided in space, they can dominate orientation perception. For example, if pressure is applied to the top of the head of an astronaut in the microgravity environment of the International Space Station, this is taken as an indication of orientation and the astronaut has a sudden feeling of standing on their head (Sangals et al. 1999). Similarly, pressure applied to the soles of the feet can reverse this sensation (Carriot et al. 2004).

Self-motion Perception in Microgravity

Moving around the International Space Station (ISS) is rather different from moving around on Earth. Astronauts typically glide from one module to another and their unloaded otoliths are stimulated only by their own acceleration (Carriot et al. 2021). Oman et al. (2003) speculated that in microgravity environments people might increase the weight given to visual cues which may then alter their experience of vection. They reported that the vection onset time of astronauts on Neurolab was reduced and that astronauts subjectively felt significantly faster motion while in microgravity compared to their pre-flight baseline. These observations were supported by Allison et al. (2012) who also found a decrease in vection onset latency when viewing smooth and jittering visual motion during brief periods of microgravity created by parabolic flight compared to when tested on Earth. Adding jitter, as explained in Section 2.4, makes the optic flow more like what would be experienced during normal walking as opposed to the smooth gliding movement experienced by astronauts moving around within the ISS. Overall, these rare studies suggest that while free floating in microgravity, people may be more sensitive to visual information for perceived self-motion due to an increased weighting of visual cues (but c.f., Harris et al. 2017a). If cues for the perception of self-motion visual and vestibular cues are integrated according to their relative reliabilities, a decrease in the reliability of the vestibular cue or a disruption of normal vestibular signalling, such as experienced in microgravity, might then lead to an increase in perceived self-motion, as measured – for example – through perceived travelled distance. McManus and Harris (2021) indeed found this expected increase in perceived travelled distance for supine observers (compared to when they were upright), particularly when they experienced a VRI in which they misperceived that they were upright. However, in experiments on the ISS (Figure 21), Jörges et al. (2024) tested astronauts' perception of how far they perceived themselves to have travelled using linear vection in a VR environment and found that their estimate of distance of self-motion, did not change significantly in response to microgravity exposure either in terms of accuracy or precision.

Figure 21 Astronaut David Saint-Jacques performing the VECTION experiment on board the International Space Station. Credits: Canadian Space Agency, NASA. The whole video is available here: https://www.asc-csa.gc.ca/eng/sciences/vection.asp.

Lunar Gravity

The Artemis program hopes to have people on the Moon in 2026 with the Lunar Gateway satellite and associated activities on the surface of the Moon following within the decade. The Moon definitely qualifies as a challenging environment. The threshold for how much gravity is needed to be useful as an orientation cue seems to show substantial inter-individual differences but is around 0.15 g (15 percent of the gravity found on Earth) as measured using a human centrifuge (Harris et al. 2014). Thus, astronauts on the Moon (which has a gravity of 0.16 g) may not be able to effectively use lunar gravity as a reliable reference for verticality (de Winkel et al. 2012). Unfortunately none of the twelve people who have actually walked on the Moon were involved in any psychophysical experiments, but lunar gravity can be created by carefully calculated parabolic flights or simulated using the NASA Johnson Space Center Space Vehicle Mock-up Facility Partial Gravity Simulator (POGO) a customized overhead suspension system that uses a pneumatic cylinder to create constant gravitational offloading (Norcross et al. 2009). A similar Lunar Analog Facility is currently under development in Cologne. Using such a lunar gravity simulator, De Witt et al. (2014) found that the transition speed at which people switch from walking to running was considerably higher than in 1G – beyond the point predicted by the inverse pendulum model for stable walking. Using parabolic flights to generate lunar gravity, de Winkel et al. (2012) confirmed that the amount of gravity needed to act as a reference for verticality was generally more than 0.16 g although Harris et al. (2012b) found that the emphasis placed on the visual cue was unaffected by lunar gravity.

6.3.4 Hypergravity

Astronauts on board a rocket on takeoff and on high-impact landings in the sea or on land experience several G. Of course, under nominal conditions they are generally not required to do anything that requires orientation or movement in such a situation. However, performance in hyperG is of theoretical interest when exploring the effects of gravity on perception in general. Clark et al. (2015) looked at the effect of up to 2G of hypergravity created using a centrifuge and found that settings of the haptic vertical suggested that otolith stimulation in the sagittal plane (see Figure 4) was processed differently than stimulation out of that plane. Research on Earth on human performance in hypergravity is typically conducted in the recovery phases of microgravity flights or using human centrifugation (Figure 22). The hyper-G phases of parabolic flights have very limited duration (~22 s) with maximum accelerations around 2-3G to avoid stress on the airframe and the passengers. Human centrifugation can

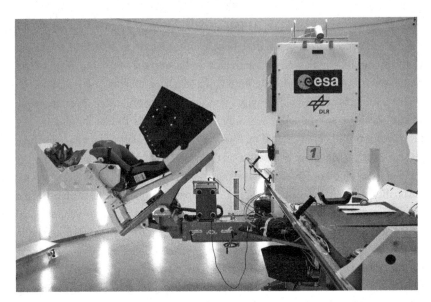

Figure 22 A human centrifuge at the DLR in Cologne. The centrifuge rotates about a vertical axis with observers are either supine – the arm on the right-hand side – or are seated in a chair that can be positioned at a range of orientations. Displays and other devices rotate with the observer.

provide much longer periods of hypergravity. However, the acceleration gradient along the radial arm of the centrifuge can be an issue. The acceleration induced at the vestibular organs is unlikely to match the acceleration induced on the liver, for example. A further complication is that human centrifugation observers must pass a very rigorous medical prior to participating in human centrifugation experiments, limiting the collection of data from all but very healthy young adults.

6.4 Summary

Challenging environments are not just the invention of human performance scientists who invent them to provide environments that expose the inner workings of human perception. They exist naturally, and these natural environments challenge the assumptions that underlie visual–vestibular information processing. From long-duration bedrest to the microgravity of outer space, these environments illustrate limitations of how we process information to solve the fundamental problems of self-orientation and self-motion perception. They also provide environments in which humans exist and must make critical decisions. Understanding how these environments impact human perception is critical for the development of countermeasures and training strategies to maximize human performance.

7 The Future

7.1 What We Think We Know and What We Think We Don't Know

Humans have adapted to successfully navigate the complex 3D environment that we inhabit (Ekstrom et al. 2018). Apart from stumbling occasionally, or bumping into a coffee table, we navigate our environment successfully. Almost always, when we place a glass on a countertop, we are successful in judging surface orientation relative to ourselves, correctly assessing grip force, moving our arm correctly and maintaining our balance while doing it! Congratulations to the multi-modal perceptual processes involved!

What makes the processes of self-motion and self-orientation perception so fascinating is how well they work in our day-to-day lives and in environments far more challenging than could possibly have been experienced in the course of our evolution. But divers drown, pilots crash, and astronauts experience disorientation and other effects that could easily imperil their lives and the success of their missions. As we have reviewed, sensorimotor integration involves both the key elements of self-orientation and self-motion. Sensory input and motor output signals are combined centrally to provide internal estimates of the state of both the world and one's own body. The state can be estimated by a process in which the internal estimate is maintained and updated by the current sensory and motor signals. The parietal lobe is critical for sensorimotor integration and for maintaining this internal representation of the body's state (Daprati et al. 2010).

Research has identified some of the limits of visual, vestibular and other sensory processing systems input to the problems of self-motion and self-orientation, but much remains to be elucidated. There are asymmetries in the processing of visual flow fields, for example in the generation of optokinetic nystagmus eye movements (van den Berg and Collewijn 1988) and the perception of vection (Fujii and Seno 2020). But much remains to be explored and understood in terms of how the visual, vestibular and other sensory systems impact perception of self-motion and self-orientation.

Advances in virtual reality (VR) technology have opened opportunities for providing complex and low-latency three-dimensional cues for self-motion and self-orientation. The complex mechanism of moving screens shown in Figure 5a are now easily replaced with commodity VR technology. Providing physical motion cues is more challenging. Although large-scale motion bases can provide controlled physical motion, they have very limited operational envelopes – especially in how far they can move and therefore for how long they can maintain an acceleration. Mechanical structures such as those sketched in Figures 8 and 10 can be used to generate much longer motion profiles, but they have their limits, both physically and from a safety point of view.

Given the relationship between gravity and the perception of self-motion and self-orientation, it becomes prudent to consider both visual and physical cues presented at different orientations relative to the direction of gravity. These have been beautifully separated by careful researchers comparing across postures (e.g., Hummel et al. 2016). Suspending an observer statically at some different angles with respect to gravity may be uncomfortable but applying maintained physical motion cues in such a plane is even more challenging.

Complicating all of this is the issue of body-centric versus head-centric frames of reference. The body is not rigidly attached to the trunk and thus a full understanding of an ego-frame involves conducting experiments with the head at different orientations relative to the body (Tarnutzer et al. 2010). Increasing somewhat the dimensionality of the experimental space. A space which is largely unexplored.

Given mechanisms to provide visual and physical motion cues, we now turn to the problem of their integration. Recent studies have demonstrated optimal integration of vestibular and visual cues (Barra et al. 2010; Cuturi and Gori 2019; Kotian et al. 2024). Neural activity in the posterior parietal cortex and vestibular nuclei reflects such an optimal combination of visual and vestibular cues for vertical perception (Bremmer et al. 2002; Delle Monache et al. 2021) and conflicting visuo-vestibular information results in perceptual disturbances (Gallagher et al. 2019, 2020). Critically, the visual and vestibular systems share multiple processing stages within the central nervous system (Mergner et al. 1989; Abekawa et al. 2018; Delle Monache et al. 2021).

Although optimal cue integration can explain much of the visual and vestibular cue-integration process, there are limits to its effectiveness. Redlick et al.'s work (2001), for example, suggests a multi-cue-integration system that seeks not to produce an optimal combination of cues in the mathematical sense, but rather a cue-combination process that optimizes something else – perhaps observer safety. As visual and vestibular cues become less and less similar – perhaps in time or the information they are providing – then a simple Bayesian integration process become less and less appropriate. But what are the properties of such a broader integration process? If we rely on multiple cue-integration processes, what are the criteria for switching from one to another? Such as from a Bayesian process to a causal inference model (Kayser and Shams 2015)? How do these processes deal with age- and injury-related changes in the visual and vestibular systems?

7.2 Some Suggestions for Future Work

A great deal of the research conducted on the perception of self-orientation and self-motion has concentrated on either visually normal or corrected-to-normal university-aged observers. Normally, their results are averaged together with the assumption that everyone is the same regardless of gender, race, socio-economic factors etc. The study of inter-individual differences and how they may impact on all aspects of perception has started (de Winkel et al. 2018b; Zanchi et al. 2022) but has a ways to go. The twenty-first century will finally see the ghost of Gibsonianism put to rest and a dominance of neural computation in describing perceptual and cognitive tasks.

7.2.1 Self-orientation

Although there has been a great deal of work on the development of multi-sensory processes (de Dieuleveult et al. 2017; Bruns and Röder 2023), relevant data are still lacking both for children and for seniors. Both sets of data are important for meeting societal needs. For example, seniors are faced with deteriorating visual and vestibular systems which are associated with gait and fall issues and even the fear of falling (Kolpashnikova et al. 2023).

Humans are remarkably effective at adapting to changes in their environment. Perhaps there is no greater environmental change than that encountered when entering the microgravity environment encountered during long-duration spaceflight. Research with astronauts on the ISS shows a remarkable ability to adapt to the environment – a process that appears to take place over a small number of days, and then to re-adapt to earth-normal conditions (Torok et al. 2019; Clément et al. 2020a). How does this adaptation process work over the small number of hours that it takes, and is adaptation associated with the space sickness that is experienced by many astronauts?

How to best prepare astronauts for landing on the Moon or Mars where they will need to make the transition from the zero G of space to an unfamiliar gravity field? What aids or training regimes will be most appropriate and useful? All are consequential questions which need to be addressed to ensure the successful future of space exploration.

7.2.2 Self-motion

Much of the work on self-motion perception has concentrated on linear or rotational motion in isolation. Yet most natural motion combines both. How does self-motion perception change with complex motion profiles, both in the plane perpendicular to gravity and when moving out of it?

Most self-motion studies assume the motion of a single observer in a stationary environment. Again, this is a simplification of natural motion in the real world. How is self-motion impacted by competing consistent or transient motion in the environment? Riddell et al. (2019), Hülemeier and Lappe (2020) have started to address these questions looking at the effects of people and other sources of biological motion in the visual field. How might extraneous motion impact the magnitude of self-motion perception?

7.2.3 Multi-cue Integration

Bayesian cue integration has proven to be an effective strategy when certain conditions are met. But the model breaks down when the visual and vestibular cues diverge or have partially correlated noise. Does there exist a formal framework that can model these properties in a compact manner?

7.2.4 The Effect of Mental Set

As mentioned several times in this Element, mental set and strategy can significantly affect perception and may significantly contribute to differences especially between active and passive paradigms. How much is the perception of motion and orientation constrained by knowledge of the experimental configuration of the apparatus, or by previous experience, or even by being told of the details of the sensory stimuli? What if such a verbal description is in conflict with the actual sensory input? Psychophysics has been carefully designed to try and avoid higher level, cognitive influences on what have traditionally been regarded as low level aspects of perception but there are clear higher level influences and this is an emerging and important area for future research (Noel and Angelaki 2022).

7.2.5 Dealing with Gravity

Finally, we come to the issue of gravity. For most humans, and for most of our lives, gravity is a constant. But for astronauts, cosmonauts and taikonauts understanding how perceptual systems are disrupted by changes in gravity from 1G to 0G, from 0G to Lunar G or back to 1G is critical for humans to operate effectively and safely. Whether a tourist on a low altitude joy ride or an astronaut returning to the Moon or heading to Mars. Understanding how gravity impacts ones' perception of self-motion and self-orientation is critical.

References

Abekawa N, Ferrè ER, Gallagher M, et al. (2018) Disentangling the visual, motor and representational effects of vestibular input. Cortex 104:46–57. https://doi.org/10.1016/j.cortex.2018.04.003.

Alais D, Burr D (2004) The ventriloquist effect results from near-optimal bimodal integration. Curr Biol CB 14:257–262. https://doi.org/10.1016/j.cub.2004.01.029.

Alberts BGT, Selen LPJ, Verhagen WIM, Medendorp WP (2015) Sensory substitution in bilateral vestibular a-reflexic patients. Physiol Rep 3:1–10. https://doi.org/10.14814/phy2.12385.

Allison R, Harris L, Hogue A (2002) Simulating self-motion ii: A virtual reality tricycle. Virtual Real 6:86–95. https://doi.org/10.1007/s100550200009.

Allison RS, Harris LR, Jenkin MR, et al. (2001) Tolerance of temporal delay in virtual environments. IEEE IntConference Virtual Real 3:247–254.

Allison RS, Howard IP, Zacher JE (1999) Effect of field size, head motion, and rotational velocity on roll vection and illusory self-tilt in a tumbling room. Perception 28:299–306.

Allison RS, Zacher JE, Kirollos R, et al. (2012) Perception of smooth and perturbed vection in short-duration microgravity. Exp Brain Res 223:479–487. https://doi.org/10.1007/s00221-012-3275-5.

Allum JHJ, Honegger F, Acuna H (1995) Differential control of leg and trunk muscle-activity by vestibulospinal and proprioceptive signals during human balance corrections. Acta Otolaryngol (Stockh) 115:124–129.

Anastasopoulos D, Bronstein A, Haslwanter T, et al. (1999) The role of somatosensory input for the perception of verticality. Ann N Y Acad Sci 871:379–383.

Anastasopoulos D, Haslwanter T, Bronstein A, et al. (1997) Dissociation between the perception of body verticality and the visual vertical in acute peripheral vestibular disorder in humans. Neurosci Lett 233:151–153.

Angelaki DE, Cullen KE (2008) Vestibular system: The many facets of a multimodal sense. Annu Rev Neurosci 31:125–150. https://doi.org/10.1146/annurev.neuro.31.060407.125555.

Angelaki DE, Dickman JD (2003) Gravity or translation: Central processing of vestibular signals to detect motion or tilt. J Vestib Res Equilib Orientat 13:245–253.

Angelaki DE, Klier EM, Snyder LH (2009) A vestibular sensation: Probabilistic approaches to spatial perception. Neuron 64:448–461. https://doi.org/10.1016/j.neuron.2009.11.010.

Angelaki DE, Wei M, Merfeld DM (2001) Vestibular discrimination of gravity and translational acceleration. Ann N Y Acad Sci 942:114–27.

Angelaki DE, Yakusheva TA (2009) How vestibular neurons solve the tilt/translation ambiguity. Comparison of brainstem, cerebellum, and thalamus. Ann N Acad Sci 1164:19–28.

Aubert H (1861) Eine scheinbare Drehung von Objekten bei Neigung des Kopfes nach rechts oder links. Virchows Arch 20:381–393.

Bansal A, McManus M, Jörges B, Harris LR (2024) Perceived travel distance depends on the speed and direction of self-motion. PLOS One 19(9): e0305661. https://doi.org/10.1371/journal.pone.0305661.

Barbot A, Xue S, Carrasco M (2021) Asymmetries in visual acuity around the visual field. J Vis 21:1–23. https://doi.org/10.1167/jov.21.1.2.

Barnett-Cowan M, Jenkin HL, Dyde RT, et al. (2013) Asymmetrical representation of body orientation. J Vis 13:1–9. https://doi.org/10.1167/13.2.3.

Barra J, Marquer A, Joassin R, et al. (2010) Humans use internal models to construct and update a sense of verticality. Brain 133:3552–3563. https://doi.org/10.1093/brain/awq311.

Barra J, Pérennou D, Thilo K V, et al. (2012) The awareness of body orientation modulates the perception of visual vertical. Neuropsychologia 50:2492–2498. https://doi.org/10.1016/j.neuropsychologia.2012.06.021.

Bauermeister M, Werner H, Wapner S (1964) The effect of body tilt on tactual-kinesthetic perception of verticality. Am J Psychol 77:451–456.

Beck B, Saramandi A, Ferrè ER, Haggard P (2020) Which way is down? Visual and tactile verticality perception in expert dancers and non-experts. Neuropsychologia 146:1–9. https://doi.org/10.1016/j.neuropsychologia.2020.107546.

Berthoz A, Pavard B, Young LR (1975) Perception of linear horizontal self-motion induced by peripheral vision (linearvection) basic characteristics and visual–vestibular interactions. Exp Brain Res 23:471–489.

Bertolini G, Ramat S, Laurens J, et al. (2011) Velocity storage contribution to vestibular self-motion perception in healthy human subjects. J Neurophysiol 105:209–223.

Betts GA, Curthoys IS (1998) Visually perceived vertical and visually perceived horizontal are not orthogonal. Vision Res 38:1989–1999. https://doi.org/10.1016/S0042-6989(97)00401-X.

Beusmans JMH (1998) Optic flow and the metric of the visual ground plane. Vis Res 38:1153–1170.

Bisdorff AR, Wolsley CJ, Anastasopoulos D, et al. (1996) The perception of body verticality (subjective postural vertical) in peripheral and central vestibular disorders. Brain 119:1523–1534. https://doi.org/10.1093/brain/119.5.1523.

Blouin J, Labrousse L, Simoneau M, et al. (1998) Updating visual space during passive and voluntary head-in-space movements. Exp Brain Res 122:93–100.

Böhmer A, Rickenmann J (1995) The subjective visual vertical as a clinical parameter of vestibular function in peripheral vestibular diseases. J Vestib Res 5:35–44.

Bortolami SB, Pierobon A, DiZio P, Lackner JR (2006a) Localization of the subjective vertical during roll, pitch, and recumbent yaw body tilt. Exp Brain Res 173:364–373.

Bortolami SB, Rocca S, Daros S, et al. (2006b) Mechanisms of human static spatial orientation. Exp Brain Res 173:374–388. https://doi.org/10.1007/s00221-006-0387-9.

Bourrelly A, McIntyre J, Luyat M (2015) Perception of affordances during long-term exposure to weightlessness in the International Space station. Cogn Process 16, Suppl 1: S171–S174. https://doi.org/10.1007/s10339-015-0692-y.

Brandt T, Dichgans JM, Koenig E (1973) Differential effects of central versus peripheral vision on egocentric and exocentric motion perception. Exp Brain Res 16:476–491.

Bray A, Subanandan A, Isableu B, et al. (2004) We are most aware of our place in the world when about to fall. Curr Biol 14:609–610. https://doi.org/10.1016/j.cub.2004.07.040.

Bremmer F, Klam F, Duhamel JR, et al. (2002) Visual–vestibular interactive responses in the macaque ventral intraparietal area (VIP). Eur J Neurosci 16:1569–1586.

Bremova T, Caushaj A, Ertl M, et al. (2016) Comparison of linear motion perception thresholds in vestibular migraine and Menière's disease. Eur Arch Otorhinolaryngol 273:2931–2939. https://doi.org/10.1007/s00405-015-3835-y.

Bringoux L, Tamura K, Faldon M, et al. (2004) Influence of whole-body pitch tilt and kinesthetic cues on the perceived gravity-referenced eye level. Exp Brain Res 155:385–392.

Brown JL (1961) Orientation to the vertical during water immersion. Aerosp Med 32:209–217.

Bruns P, Röder B (2023) Development and experience-dependence of multisensory spatial processing. Trends Cogn Sci 27:961–973. https://doi.org/10.1016/j.tics.2023.04.012.

Buck LE, Young MK, Bodenheimer B (2018) A comparison of distance estimation in HMD-based virtual environments with different HMD-based conditions. ACM Trans Appl Percept 15: Article 21, 1–15. https://doi.org/10.1145/3196885.

Buckey JC, Homick JL (2003) Neurolab Spacelab Mission: Neuroscience Research in Space, Results from the STS-90, Neurolab Spacelab Mission. Lyndon B. Johnson Space Center, Houston.

Burles F, Willson M, Townes P, et al. (2024) Preliminary evidence of high prevalence of cerebral microbleeds in astronauts with spaceflight experience. Front Physiol 15:1–13. https://doi.org/10.3389/fphys.2024.1360353.

Bury NA, Jenkin M, Allison RS, et al. (2023) Vection underwater illustrates the limitations of neutral buoyancy as a microgravity analog. Npj Microgravity 9:1–10. https://doi.org/10.1038/s41526-023-00282-3.

Carpenter-Smith TR, Futamura RG, Parker DE (1995) Inertial acceleration as a measure of linear vection: An alternative to magnitude estimation. Percept Psychophys 57:35–42.

Carriot J, Bringoux L, Charles C, et al. (2004) Perceived body orientation in microgravity: Effects of prior experience and pressure under the feet. Aviat Space Env Med 75:795–799.

Carriot J, Brooks JX, Cullen KE (2013) Multimodal integration of self-motion cues in the vestibular system: Active versus passive translations. J Neurosci Off J Soc Neurosci 33:19555–19566. https://doi.org/10.1523/JNEUROSCI.3051-13.2013.

Carriot J, Jamali M, Cullen KE (2015) Rapid adaptation of multisensory integration in vestibular pathways. Front Syst Neurosci 9:1–5. https://doi.org/10.3389/fnsys.2015.00059.

Carriot J, Mackrous I, Cullen KE (2021) Challenges to the vestibular system in space: How the brain responds and adapts to microgravity. Front Neural Circuits 15:1–12. https://doi.org/10.3389/fncir.2021.760313.

Chang C-H, Stoffregen TA, Lei MK, et al. (2024) Effects of decades of physical driving experience on pre-exposure postural precursors of motion sickness among virtual passengers. Front Virtual Real 5:1–12. https://doi.org/10.3389/frvir.2024.1258548.

Clark TK (2019) Effects of spaceflight on the vestibular system. In Pathak Y, Araùjo dos Santos M, Zea L (eds) Handbook of Space Pharmaceuticals. Springer, Cham. pp. 1–39.

Clark TK, Newman MC, Oman CM, et al. (2015) Human perceptual overestimation of whole body roll tilt in hypergravity. J Neurophysiol 113:2062–2077. https://doi.org/10.1152/jn.00095.2014.

Clemens IA, De Vrijer M, Selen LPJ, et al. (2011) Multisensory processing in spatial orientation: An inverse probabilistic approach. J Neurosci 31:5365–5377.

Clément G, Berthoz A, Cohen B, et al. (2003) Perception of the spatial vertical during centrifugation and static tilt. In Buckley J, Homick J (eds) The Neurolab Spacelab Mission: Neuroscience Research in Space. NASA, Houston, pp. 5–10.

Clément G, Boyle RD, George KA, et al. (2020a) Challenges to the central nervous system during human spaceflight missions to Mars. J Neurophysiol 123:2037–2063. https://doi.org/10.1152/jn.00476.2019.

Clément G, Bukley A, Loureiro N, et al. (2020b) Horizontal and vertical distance perception in altered gravity. Sci Rep 10:1–11. https://doi.org/10.1038/s41598-020-62405-0.

Clément G, Moore SJ, Raphan T, Cohen B (2001) Perception of tilt (somatogravic illusion) in response to sustained linear acceleration during space flight. Exp Brain Res 138:410–418. https://doi.org/10.1007/s002210100706.

Convertino VA, Bloomfield SA, Greenleaf JE (1997) An overview of the issues: Physiological effects of bed rest and restricted physical activity. Med Sci Sports Exerc 29:187–190. https://doi.org/10.1097/00005768-199702000-00004.

Corballis MC, Zbrodoff NJ, Shetzer LI, Butler PB (1978) Decisions about identity and orientation of rotated letters and digits. Mem Cogn 6:98–107.

Correia MJ, Hixson WC, Niven JI (1968) On predictive equations for subjective judgments of vertical and horizon in a force field. Acta Otolaryngol Suppl 230:1–20.

Creem-Regehr SH, Stefanucci JK, Bodenheimer B (2023) Perceiving distance in virtual reality: Theoretical insights from contemporary technologies. Philos Trans R Soc B Biol Sci 378:1–12. https://doi.org/10.1098/rstb.2021.0456.

Curthoys IS (1996) The role of ocular torsion in visual measures of vestibular function. Brain Res Bull 40:404–405.

Cuturi LF, Gori M (2019) Biases in the visual and haptic subjective vertical reveal the role of proprioceptive/vestibular priors in child development. Front Neurol 10:1–10. https://doi.org/10.3389/fneur.2018.01151.

Daprati E, Sirigu A, Nico D (2010) Body and movement: Consciousness in the parietal lobes. Neuropsychologia 48:756–762. https://doi.org/10.1016/j.neuropsychologia.2009.10.008.

De Beer GR (1947) How animals hold their heads. Proc Linn Soc 159:125–139.

de Dieuleveult AL, Siemonsma PC, van Erp JBF, Brouwer A-M (2017) Effects of aging in multisensory integration: A systematic review. Front Aging Neurosci 9:1–14. https://doi.org/10.3389/fnagi.2017.00080.

de Winkel KN, Clément G, Groen EL, Werkhoven PJ (2012) The perception of verticality in lunar and Martian gravity conditions. Neurosci Lett 529:7–11.

de Winkel KN, Katliar M, Diers D, Bülthoff HH (2018a) Causal inference in the perception of verticality. Sci Rep 8:1–12. https://doi.org/10.1038/s41598-018-23838-w.

de Winkel KN, Kurtz M, Bülthoff HH (2018b) Effects of visual stimulus characteristics and individual differences in heading estimation. J Vis 18:1–17. https://doi.org/10.1167/18.11.9.

De Witt JK, Edwards WB, Scott-Pandorf MM, et al. (2014) The preferred walk to run transition speed in actual lunar gravity. J Exp Biol 217:3200–3203. https://doi.org/10.1242/jeb.105684.

Delle Monache S, Indovina I, Zago M, et al. (2021) Watching the effects of gravity. Vestibular cortex and the neural representation of "visual" gravity. Front Integr Neurosci 15: 1–17.

Dyde RT, Jenkin MR, Harris LR (2006) The subjective visual vertical and the perceptual upright. Exp Brain Res 173:612–622.

Einstein A (1908) Über das Relativitätsprinzip und die aus dem selben gezogenen Folgerungen. Jahrb Radioakt 4:411–462.

Ekstrom, A, Spiers HJ, Bohbot VD, Rosenbaum RS (2018) Human Spatial Navigation. Princeton University Press, Princeton, NJ.

Ernst MO, Banks MS (2002) Humans integrate visual and haptic information in a statistically optimal fashion. Nature 415:429–433. https://doi.org/10.1038/415429a.

Evans L, Champion RA, Rushton SK, Warren PA (2020) Detection of scene-relative object movement and optic flow parsing across the adult lifespan. J Vis 20(9):12:1–18.

Fajen BR, Warren WH (2000) Go with the flow. Trends Cogn Sci 4:369–370.

Fauville G, Queiroz ACM, Woolsey ES, et al. (2021) The effect of water immersion on vection in virtual reality. Sci Rep 11:1–13. https://doi.org/10.1038/s41598-020-80100-y.

Fernandez C, Goldberg JM (1976) Physiology of peripheral neurons innervating otolith organs of the squirrel monkey. II. Directional selectivity and force-response relations. J Neurophysiol 39:985–995.

Fetter M, Haslwanter T, Misslisch H, Tweed D (1997) Three-dimensional kinematics of eye, head and limb movements. Harwood Academic, Amsterdam.

Fraser LE, Makooie B, Harris LR (2015) The subjective visual vertical and the subjective haptic vertical access different gravity estimates. PLOS One 10:1–20.

Frenz H, Lappe M (2005) Absolute travel distance from optic flow. Vision Res 45:1679–1692. https://doi.org/10.1016/j.visres.2004.12.019.

Frisby, JP. (2010) Seeing: The computational approach to biological vision, 2nd ed. MIT Press, Boston, MA.

Frith CD, Blakemore SJ, Wolpert DM (2000) Abnormalities in the awareness and control of action. Philos Trans R Soc Lond B Biol Sci 355:1771–1788.

Fujii Y, Seno T (2020) The effect of optical flow motion direction on vection strength. Perception 11:1–13. https://doi.org/10.1177/2041669519899108.

Gallagher M, Arshad I, Ferrè ER (2019) Gravity modulates behaviour control strategy. Exp Brain Res 237:989–994. https://doi.org/10.1007/s00221-019-05479-1.

Gallagher M, Choi R, Ferrà ER (2020) Multisensory interactions in virtual reality: Optic flow reduces vestibular sensitivity, but only for congruent planes of motion. Multisensory Res 33:625–644. https://doi.org/10.1163/22134808-20201487.

Gianna C, Heimbrand S, Gresty M, et al. (1996) Thresholds for detection of motion direction during passive lateral whole-body acceleration in normal subjects and patients with bilateral loss of labyrinthine function. Brain Res Bull 40:443–449.

Gibb R, Ercoline B, Scharff L (2011) Spatial disorientation: Decades of pilot fatalities. Aviat Space Environ Med 82:717–724. https://doi.org/10.3357/asem.3048.2011.

Gibson JJ (1950) The Perception of the Visual World. Houghton Mifflin, Boston.

Gibson JJ (1966) The Senses Considered as Perceptual Systems. Houghton Mifflin, Boston.

Girshick AR, Banks MS (2009) Probabilistic combination of slant information: Weighted averaging and robustness as optimal percepts. J Vis 9:1–36. https://doi.org/10.1167/9.9.8.

Glass SM, Rhea CK, Wittstein MW, et al. (2018) Changes in posture following a single session of long-duration water immersion. J Appl Biomech 34:435–441. https://doi.org/10.1123/jab.2017-0181.

Goodale MA, Milner AD (1992) Separate visual pathways for perception and action. Trends Neurosci 15:20–25.

Goodale MA, Milner AD (2018) Two visual pathways – Where have they taken us and where will they lead in future? Cortex 98:283–292. https://doi.org/10.1016/j.cortex.2017.12.002.

Grassi M, Von Der Straten F, Pearce C, et al. (2024) Changes in real-world walking speed following 60-day bed-rest. Npj Microgravity 10:1–12. https://doi.org/10.1038/s41526-023-00342-8.

Graybiel A (1952) The oculogravic illusion. Am Med Assoc Arch Ophthalmol 48:605–615.

Graybiel A, Patterson JL (1955) Thresholds of stimulation of the otolith organs as indicated by the oculogravic illusion. J Appl Physiol 7:666–670.

Green AM, Angelaki DE (2003) Resolution of sensory ambiguities for gaze stabilization requires a second neural integrator. J Neurosci 23:9265–9275.

Guedes LPCM, Oliveira MLCD, Carvalho GDA (2018) Deleterious effects of prolonged bed rest on the body systems of the elderly – a review. Rev Bras Geriatr E Gerontol 21:499–506. https://doi.org/10.1590/1981-22562018021.170167.

Hargens AR, Vico L (2016) Long-duration bed rest as an analog to microgravity. J Appl Physiol 120:891–903. https://doi.org/10.1152/japplphysiol.00935.2015.

Harris LR, Herpers R, Hofhammer T, Jenkin MR (2014) How much gravity is needed to establish the perceptual upright? PLOS One 9:1–7. https://doi.org/10.1371/journal.pone.0106207.

Harris LR, Herpers R, Jenkin M, et al. (2012a) The relative contributions of radial and laminar optic flow to the perception of linear self-motion. J Vis 12:1–10. https://doi.org/10.1167/12.10.7.

Harris LR, Jenkin MR, Dyde RT (2012b) The perception of upright under lunar gravity. J Gravitational Physiol 2:9–16.

Harris LR, Jenkin M, Herpers R (2022) Long-duration head down bed rest as an analog of microgravity: Effects on the static perception of upright. J Vestib Res 32:325–340. https://doi.org/10.3233/VES-210016.

Harris LR, Jenkin M, Jenkin H, et al. (2017a) The effect of long-term exposure to microgravity on the perception of upright. Npj Microgravity 3:1–8. https://doi.org/10.1038/s41526-016-0005-5.

Harris LR, Jenkin MR, Zikovitz DC (2000) Visual and non-visual cues in the perception of linear self motion. Exp Brain Res 135:12–21. https://doi.org/10.1007/s002210000504.

Harris LR, Sakurai K, Beaudot WHA (2017b) Tactile flow overrides other cues to self motion. Sci Rep 7:1–8. https://doi.org/10.1038/s41598-017-01111-w.

Hecht H, Brendel E, Wessels M, Bernhard C (2021) Estimating time-to-contact when vision is impaired. Sci Rep 11:1–14. https://doi.org/10.1038/s41598-021-00331-5.

Helland A, Lydersen S, Lervåg L-E, et al. (2016) Driving simulator sickness: Impact on driving performance, influence of blood alcohol concentration, and effect of repeated simulator exposures. Accid Anal Prev 94:180–187. https://doi.org/10.1016/j.aap.2016.05.008.

Helmholtz H von. (1866) Handbuch der physiologischen Optik (Handbook of Physiological Optics). Voss, Leipzig.

Hershberger W (1970) Attached-shadow orientation perceived as depth by chickens reared in an environment illuminated from below. J Comp Physiol Psychol 73:407–411.

Hollands MA, Patla AE, Vickers JN (2002) "Look where you're going!": Gaze behaviour associated with maintaining and changing the direction of locomotion. Exp Brain Res Exp Hirnforsch Expérimentation Cérébrale 143:221–230. https://doi.org/10.1007/s00221-001-0983-7.

Holst E, Mittelstaedt H (1971) The principle of reafference: Interactions between the central nervous system and the peripheral organs. PC Dodwell Ed Trans Percept Process Stimul Equiv Pattern Recognit 41–72.

Howard IP (1982) Human Visual Orientation. John Wiley, New York.

Howard IP, Bergstrom SS, Ohmi M (1990) Shape from shading in different frames of reference. Perception 19:523–530.

Hülemeier AG, Lappe M (2020) Combining biological motion perception with optic flow analysis for self-motion in crowds. J Vis 20:1–15. https://doi.org/10.1167/JOV.20.9.7.

Hummel N, Cuturi LF, MacNeilage PR, Flanagin VL (2016) The effect of supine body position on human heading perception. J Vis 16:1–11. https://doi.org/10.1167/16.3.19.

Israël I, Fetter M, Koenig E (1993) Vestibular perception of passive whole-body rotation about horizontal and vertical axes in humans: Goal-directed vestibulo-ocular reflex and vestibular memory-contingent saccades. Exp Brain Res 96:335–346. https://doi.org/10.1007/BF00227113.

Iwase S, Nishimura N, Tanaka K, et al. (2020) Effects of microgravity on human physiology. In Beyond LEO: Human Health Issues for Deep Space Exploration. IntechOpen. http://dx.doi.org/10.5772/intechopen.90700.

Jenkin HL, Jenkin MR, Dyde RT, Harris LR (2004) Shape-from-shading depends on visual, gravitational, and body-orientation cues. Perception 33:1453–1461.

Jenkin HL, Jenkin M, Harris LR, Herpers R (2023) Neutral buoyancy and the static perception of upright. Npj Microgravity 9:1–7. https://doi.org/10.1038/s41526-023-00296-x.

Joassin R, Bonniaud V, Barra J, et al. (2010) Somaesthetic perception of the vertical in spinal cord injured patients: A clinical study. Ann Phys Rehabil Med 53:568–574. https://doi.org/10.1016/j.rehab.2010.07.005.

Jörges B, Bury N, McManus M, et al. (2024) The effects of long-term exposure to microgravity and body orientation relative to gravity on perceived traveled distance. Npj Microgravity 10:1–8. https://doi.org/10.1038/s41526-024-00376-6.

Kayser C, Shams L (2015) Multisensory causal inference in the brain. PLoS Biol 13:1–7. https://doi.org/10.1371/journal.pbio.1002075.

Kleffner DA, Ramachandran VS (1992) On the perception of shape from shading. Percept Psychophys 52:18–36.

Knill DC (2007) Robust cue integration: A Bayesian model and evidence from cue-conflict studies with stereoscopic and figure cues to slant. J Vis 7:1–24. https://doi.org/10.1167/7.7.5.

Kobel MJ, Wagner AR, Merfeld DM (2021) Impact of gravity on the perception of linear motion. J Neurophysiol 126:875–887. https://doi.org/10.1152/jn.00274.2021.

Kobel MJ, Wagner AR, Merfeld DM (2024) Vestibular contributions to linear motion perception. Exp Brain Res 242:385–402. https://doi.org/10.1007/s00221-023-06754-y.

Kolpashnikova K, Harris LR, Desai S (2023) Fear of falling: Scoping review and topic analysis using natural language processing. PLOS One 18:1–19. https://doi.org/10.1371/journal.pone.0293554.

Kooijman L, Berti S, Asadi H, et al. (2024) Measuring vection: A review and critical evaluation of different methods for quantifying illusory self-motion. Behav Res Methods 56:2292–2310. https://doi.org/10.3758/s13428-023-02148-8.

Körding KP, Beierholm UR, Ma WJ, et al. (2007) Causal inference in multi-sensory perception. PLOS One 2:1–10.

Kotian V, Irmak T, Pool D, Happee R (2024) The role of vision in sensory integration models for predicting motion perception and sickness. Exp Brain Res 242:685–725. https://doi.org/10.1007/s00221-023-06747-x.

Krala M, van Kemenade B, Straube B, et al. (2019) Predictive coding in a multisensory path integration task: An fMRI study. J Vis 19:1–15. https://doi.org/10.1167/19.11.13.

Lackner JR, DiZio P (2000) Human orientation and movement control in weightless and artificial gravity environments. Exp Brain Res 130:2–26.

Lackner JR, Dizio P (2006) Space motion sickness. Exp Brain Res 175:377–399. https://doi.org/10.1007/s00221-006-0697-y.

Lake A (1893) Illusion Apparatus. US Patent 508227.

Landwehr K, Brendel E, Hecht H (2013) Luminance and contrast in visual perception of time to collision. Vision Res 89:18–23. https://doi.org/10.1016/j.visres.2013.06.009.

Landy MS, Maloney LT, Johnston EB, Young M (1995) Measurement and modeling of depth cue combination: In defense of weak fusion. Vision Res 35:389–412. https://doi.org/10.1016/0042-6989(94)00176-M.

Lappe M, Jenkin M, Harris LR (2007) Travel distance estimation from visual motion by leaky path integration. Exp Brain Res 180:35–48. https://doi.org/10.1007/s00221-006-0835-6.

Latash ML (2021) Efference copy in kinesthetic perception: A copy of what is it? J Neurophysiol 125:1079–1094. https://doi.org/10.1152/jn.00545.2020.

Laurens J, Angelaki DE (2017) A unified internal model theory to resolve the paradox of active versus passive self-motion sensation. eLife 6:1–45. https://doi.org/10.7554/eLife.28074.

Lechner-Steinleitner S, Schone H (1980) The subjective vertical under "dry" and "wet" conditions at clockwise and counterclockwise changed positions and the effect of a parallel-lined background field. Psychol Res 41:305–317.

Liegeois-Chauvel C, Musolino A, Chauvel P (1991) Localization of the primary auditory area in man. Brain 114:139–153.

Lobmaier JS, Mast FW (2007) The Thatcher illusion: Rotating the viewer instead of the picture. Perception 36:537–546.

Longuet-Higgins HC, Prazdny K (1980) The interpretation of a moving retinal image. Proceeding R Soc Lond 208:385–397.

Mach E (1875) Grundlinien der Lehre von den Bewegungsempfindungen. W. Engelmann, Leipzig.

Mackenzie SW, Smith CP, Tremblay MF, et al. (2024) Bed rest impairs the vestibular control of balance. J Physiol. 602:2985–2998. https://doi.org/10.1113/JP285834.

MacNeilage PR, Banks MS, Berger DR, Bülthoff HH (2007) A Bayesian model of the disambiguation of gravitoinertial force by visual cues. Exp Brain Res 179:263–290.

MacNeilage PR, Banks MS, DeAngelis GC, Angelaki DE (2010) Vestibular heading discrimination and sensitivity to linear acceleration in head and world coordinates. J Neurosci 30:9084–9094.

Macuga KL, Beall AC, Smith RS, Loomis JM (2019) Visual control of steering in curve driving. J Vis 19:1–12. https://doi.org/10.1167/19.5.1.

Mamassian P, Goutcher R (2001) Prior knowledge on the illumination position. Cognition 81:B1–B9.

Mast FW, Jarchow T (1996) Perceived body position and the visual horizontal. Brain Res Bull 40:393–398.

Mast FW, Kosslyn SM, Berthoz A (1999) Visual mental imagery interferes with allocentric orientation judgements. Cogn Neurosci 10:3549–3553.

Mayo AM, Wade MG, Stoffregen TA (2011) Postural effects of the horizon on land and at sea. Psychol Sci 22:118–124. https://doi.org/10.1177/0956797610392927.

McCarthy J, Castro P, Cottier R, et al. (2021) Multisensory contribution in visuo-spatial orientation: An interaction between neck and trunk proprioception. Exp Brain Res 239:2501–2508. https://doi.org/10.1007/s00221-021-06146-0.

McManus M, Harris LR (2021) When gravity is not where it should be: How perceived orientation affects visual self-motion processing. PLOS One 16:1–24. https://doi.org/10.1371/journal.pone.0243381.

McMullen PA, Jolicoeur P (1992) Reference frame and effects of orientation of finding the tops of rotated objects. J Exp Psychol Hum Perc Perf 3:807–820.

Melvill Jones G, Spells KE (1963) A theoretical and comparative study of the functional dependence of the semicircular canal upon its physical dimensions. Proc R Soc Lond B Biol Sci 157:403–419. https://doi.org/10.1098/rspb.1963.0019.

Merfeld DM (2003) Rotation otolith tilt-translation reinterpretation (ROTTR) hypothesis: A new hypothesis to explain neurovestibular spaceflight adaptation. J Vestib Res Equilib Orientat 13:309–320.

Merfeld DM, Park S, Gianna-Poulin C, et al. (2005a) Vestibular perception and action employ qualitatively different mechanisms. I. Frequency response of VOR and perceptual responses during translation and tilt. J Neurophysiol 94:186–198. https://doi.org/10.1152/jn.00904.2004.

Merfeld DM, Park S, Gianna-Poulin C, et al. (2005b) Vestibular perception and action employ qualitatively different mechanisms. II. VOR and perceptual responses during combined Tilt&Translation. J Neurophysiol 94:199–205.

Merfeld DM, Zupan L, Peterka RJ (1999) Humans use internal models to estimate gravity and linear acceleration. Nature 398:615–618. https://doi.org/10.1038/19303.

Mergner T, Schrenk R, Muller C (1989) Human DC scalp potentials during vestibular and optokinetic stimulation – non-specific responses. Electroencephalogr Clin Neurophysiol 73:322–333.

Mertz S, Lepecq JC (1998) Test of a vestibular imagery in man – interaction between imagery and perception. Eur J Neurosci 10:15109.

Mittelstaedt H (1983) A new solution to the problem of the subjective vertical. Naturwissenschaften 70:272–281.

Mittelstaedt H (1996) Somatic graviception. Biol Psychol 42:53–74.

Mittelstaedt H (1999) The role of the otoliths in perception of the vertical and in path integration. Ann N Y Acad Sci 871:334–344.

Morgenstern Y, Murray RM, Harris LR (2011) The human visual system's assumption that light comes from above is weak. Proceeding Natl Acad Sci 108:12551–12553. https://doi.org/10.1073/pnas.1100794108.

Mueller AS, Timney B (2016) Visual acceleration perception for simple and complex motion patterns. PLOS One 11:1–10. https://doi.org/10.1371/jour nal.pone.0149413.

Müller GE (1918) Über das Aubertsche Phënomen. Z Sinnesphysiol 49:109–246.

Mündermann L, Corazza S, Andriacchi TP (2006) The evolution of methods for the capture of human movement leading to markerless motion capture for biomechanical applications. J NeuroEngineering Rehabil 3:1–11. https://doi.org/10.1186/1743-0003-3-6.

Murata K, Seno T, Ozawa Y, Ichihara S (2014) Self-motion perception induced by cutaneous sensation caused by constant wind. Psychology 5:1777–1782.

Murovec B, Spaniol J, Campos JL, Keshavarz B (2021) Multisensory effects on illusory self-motion (Vection): The role of visual, auditory, and tactile cues. Multisensory Res 34:869–890. https://doi.org/10.1163/22134808-bja10058.

Nakamura J, Shiozaki T, Tsujimoto N, et al. (2020) Role of somatosensory and/ or vestibular sensory information in subjective postural vertical in healthy adults. Neurosci Lett 714:1–5. https://doi.org/10.1016/j.neulet.2019.134598.

Naval Air Training Command (2002) Joint Aerospace Physiology Student Guide. Corpus Chrisi, Texas.

Navarro Morales DC, Kuldavletova O, Quarck G, et al. (2023) Time perception in astronauts on board the International Space Station. Npj Microgravity 9:1–7. https://doi.org/10.1038/s41526-023-00250-x.

Negishi K, Borowski AG, Popović ZB, et al. (2017) Effect of gravitational gradi-ents on cardiac filling and performance. J Am Soc Echocardiogr 30:1180–1188. https://doi.org/10.1016/j.echo.2017.08.005.

Neufeld MJ, Charles JB (2015) Practicing for space underwater: Inventing neutral buoyancy training, 1963–1968. Endeavour 39:147–159. https://doi.org/10.1016/j.endeavour.2015.05.006.

Niehorster DC, Li L (2017) Accuracy and tuning of flow parsing for visual perception of object motion during self-motion. i-Perception 8:1–18. https://doi.org/10.1177/2041669517708206.

Noel J, Angelaki DE (2022) Cognitive, systems, and computational neurosci-ences of the self in motion. Annu Rev Psychol 73:8.1–8.27. https://doi.org/10.1146/annurev-psych-021021-103038.

Noel J-P, Bill J, Ding H, et al. (2023) Causal inference during closed-loop navigation: Parsing of self- and object-motion. Philos Trans R Soc B Biol Sci 378:1–13. https://doi.org/10.1098/rstb.2022.0344.

Norcross J, Lee L, Witt JKD, et al. (2009) Feasibility of Suited 10-km Ambulation "Walkback" on the Moon. Final Rep EVA Walkback Test EWT Hanover MD NASA Tech Rep TP-2009–214796.

Oman CM (2003) Human visual orientation in weightlessness. In Harris LR, Jenkin M (eds) Levels of Perception. Springer-Verlag, New York, pp. 375–398.

Oman CM (2007) Spatial orientation and navigation in microgravity. In Mast FW, Jänke L (eds) Spatial Processing in Navigation, Imagery and Perception. Springer, New York, pp. 209–248.

Oman CM, Howard IP, Smith T, et al. (2003) The role of visual cues in microgravity spatial orientation. Neurolab Spacelab Mission 69–81.

Paez YM, Mudie LI, Subramanian PS (2020) Spaceflight associated neuro-ocular syndrome (Sans): A systematic review and future directions. Eye Brain 12:105–117. https://doi.org/10.2147/EB.S234076.

Palmisano S, Allison RS, Ash A, et al. (2014) Evidence against an ecological explanation of the jitter advantage for vection. Front Psychol 5:1–9. https://doi.org/10.3389/fpsyg.2014.01297.

Palmisano S, Allison RS, Kim J, Bonato F (2011) Simulated viewpoint jitter shakes sensory conflict accounts of vection. Seeing Perceiving 24:173–200. https://doi.org/10.1163/187847511X570817.

Palmisano S, Gillam BJ, Blackburn SG (2000) Global-perspective jitter improves vection in central vision. Perception 29:57–67. https://doi.org/10.1068/p2990.

Parker DE, Reschke MF, Arrott AP, et al. (1985) Otolith tilt-translation reinterpretation following prolonged weightlessness – implications for preflight training. Aviat Space Environ Med 56:601–606.

Pleshkov M, Rondas N, Lucieer F, et al. (2022) Reported thresholds of self-motion perception are influenced by testing paradigm. J Neurol. 269: 5755–5761. https://doi.org/10.1007/s00415-022-11032-y.

Pokorny, J, Smith, VC (2020) Fifty years exploring the visual system. Annu Rev Vis Sci 6:1–23. https://doi.org/10.1146/annurev-vision-121219-081824.

Previc FH, Ercoline WR (2004) Spatial disorientation in aviation. In Vol 203 Progress in Astronautics and Aeronautics. American Institute of Aeronautics and Astronautics, Inc, Reston, Virginia, USA.

Ramachandran VS (1988) The perception of shape from shading. Nature 331:163–166.

Rasmussen R, Cole J, Kuperman M, Moore R (2000) Common snowfall conditions associated with aircraft takeoff accidents. J Aircr – J Aircr 37:110–116. https://doi.org/10.2514/2.2568.

Rebenitsch L, Owen C (2016) Review on cybersickness in applications and visual displays. Virtual Real 20:101–125. https://doi.org/10.1007/s10055-016-0285-9.

Redlick FP, Jenkin M, Harris LR (2001) Humans can use optic flow to estimate distance of travel. Vision Res 41:213–219.

Riccio GE, Stoffregen TA (1991) An ecological theory of motion sickness and postural instability. Ecol Psychol 3:195–240. https://doi.org/10.1207/s15326969eco0303_2.

Riddell H, Li L, Lappe M (2019) Heading perception from optic flow in the presence of biological motion. J Vis 19:1–14. https://doi.org/10.1167/19.14.25.

Riecke BE, Murovec B, Campos JL, Keshavarz B (2023) Beyond the eye: Multisensory contributions to the sensation of illusory self-motion (vection). Multisensory Res 36:827–864. https://doi.org/10.1163/22134808-bja10112.

Rineau A-L, Bringoux L, Sarrazin J-C, Berberian B (2023) Being active over one's own motion: Considering predictive mechanisms in self-motion perception. Neurosci Biobehav Rev 146:1–19. https://doi.org/10.1016/j.neubiorev.2023.105051.

Rock I, Heimer W (1957) The effect of retinal and phenomenal orientation on the perception of form. Am J Psychol 70:493–511.

Rock I, Schreiber C, Ro T (1994) The dependence of two-dimensional shape perception on orientation. Perception 23:1409–1426.

Rodriguez R, Crane BT (2021) Effect of timing delay between visual and vestibular stimuli on heading perception. J Neurophysiol 126: 304–312. https://doi.org/10.1152/jn.00351.2020.

Rogers B (2021) Optic flow: Perceiving and acting in a 3-D world. i-Percept 12:1–25. https://doi.org/10.1177/2041669520987257.

Rosas P, Wagemans J, Ernst MO, Wichmann FA (2005) Texture and haptic cues in slant discrimination: Reliability-based cue weighting without statistically optimal cue combination. J Opt Soc Am A 22:801–809. https://doi.org/10.1364/JOSAA.22.000801.

Roy JE, Cullen KE (2001) Selective processing of vestibular reafference during self-generated head motion. J Neurosci Off J Soc Neurosci 21:2131–2142.

Rupert AH, Lawson BD, Basso JE (2016) Tactile Situation Awareness System: Recent developments for aviation. Proc Hum Factors Ergon Soc Annual Meeting. 721–725. https://doi.org/10.1177/1541931213601165.

Sangals J, Heuer H, Manzey D, Lorenz B (1999) Changed visuomotor transformations during and after prolonged microgravity. Exp Brain Res 129:378–390. https://doi.org/10.1007/s002210050906.

Schmitt C, Krala M, Bremmer F (2022) Neural signatures of actively controlled self-motion and the subjective encoding of distance. eNeuro 9:1–18. https://doi.org/10.1523/ENEURO.0137-21.2022.

Schuler JR, Bockisch CJ, Straumann D, Tarnutzer AA (2010) Precision and accuracy of the subjective haptic vertical in the roll plane. BMC Neurosci 11:1–11.

Seno T, Ogawa M, Ito H, Sunaga S (2011) Consistent air flow to the face facilitates vection. Perception 40:1237–1240.

Shaikh D (2022) Learning multisensory cue integration: A computational model of crossmodal synaptic plasticity enables reliability-based cue weighting by capturing stimulus statistics. Front Neural Circuits 16:1–19. https://doi.org/10.3389/fncir.2022.921453.

Shams L, Beierholm UR (2010) Causal inference in perception. Trends Cogn Sci 14:425–432. https://doi.org/10.1016/j.tics.2010.07.001.

Sinnott C, Liu J, Matera C, et al. (2019) Underwater Virtual Reality System for Neutral Buoyancy Training: Development and Evaluation. In 25th ACM Symposium on Virtual Reality Software and Technology. ACM, Parramatta NSW Australia, pp 1–9.

Snowden RJ, Stimpson N, Ruddle RA (1998) Speed perception fogs up as visibility drops. Nature 392:450.

Srinivasan MV, Zang S, Bidwell N (1997) Visually mediated odometry in honeybees. J Exp Biol 200:2513–2522.

Stetson C, Cui X, Montague PR, Eagleman DM (2006) Motor-sensory recalibration leads to an illusory reversal of action and sensation. Neuron 51:651–659. https://doi.org/10.1016/j.neuron.2006.08.006.

Stoffregen TA. , Mantel B, Bardy BG (2017). The senses considered as one perceptual system. Ecol Psychol 29:165–197. https://doi.org/10.1080/10407413.2017.1331116.

Stoffregen TA, Chen F-C, Varlet M, et al. (2013) Getting your sea legs. PLOS One 8:1–16. https://doi.org/doi:10.1371/journal.pone.0066949.

Stoffregen TA, Riccio GE (1988) An ecological theory of orientation and the vestibular system. Psychol Rev 95:3–14.

Stürzel F, Spillmann L (2000) Thatcher illusion: Dependence on angle of rotation. Perception 29:937–942. https://doi.org/10.1068/p2888.

Sylvestre PA, Choi JT, Cullen KE (2003) Discharge dynamics of oculomotor neural integrator neurons during conjugate and disjunctive saccades and fixation. J Neurophysiol 90:739–754.

Tarnutzer AA, Bockisch CJ, Straumann D (2010) Roll-dependent modulation of the subjective visual vertical: Contributions of head-and trunk-based signals. J Neurophysiol 103:934–941. https://doi.org/10.1152/jn.00407.2009.

Tarnutzer AA, Bockisch C, Straumann D, Olasagasti I (2009) Gravity dependence of subjective visual vertical variability. J Neurophysiol 102:1657–1671. https://doi.org/10.1152/jn.00007.2008.

Taylor JL (1992) Perception of the orientation of the head on the body in man. In Berthoz A, Graf W, Vidal PP (eds) The Head-Neck Sensory Motor System. Oxford University Press, Oxford, pp. 488–490.

Teaford M, Mularczyk ZJ, Gernon A, et al. (2023) Joint contributions of auditory, proprioceptive and visual cues on human balance. Multisensory Res 36:865–890. https://doi.org/10.1163/22134808-bja10113.

Teixeira J, Miellet S, Palmisano S (2024) Effects of vection type and postural instability on cybersickness. Virtual Real 28:1–18. https://doi.org/10.1007/s10055-024-00969-2.

Telford L, Frost BJ (1993) Factors affecting the onset and magnitude of linear vection. Percept Psychophys 53:682–692.

Telford L, Howard IP, Ohmi M (1995) Heading judgments during active and passive self-motion. Exp Brain Res 104:502–510. https://doi.org/10.1007/BF00231984.

Thompson P (1980) Margaret Thatcher: A new illusion. Perception 9:483–484.

Torok A, Gallagher M, Lasbareilles C, Ferrè ER (2019) Getting ready for Mars: How the brain perceives new simulated gravitational environments. Q J Exp Psychol 72:2342–2349. https://doi.org/10.1177/1747021819839962.

Tribukait A (2006) Subjective visual horizontal in the upright posture and asymmetry in roll-tilt perception: Independent measures of vestibular function. J Vestib Res 16:35–43.

Trout OF (1967) Water immersion simulation of extravehicular activities by astronauts. J Spacecr Rockets 4:806–808. https://doi.org/10.2514/3.28960.

Tsakiris M (2010) My body in the brain: A neurocognitive model of body-ownership. Neuropsychologia 48:703–712.

Tsakiris M, Costantini M, Haggard P (2008) The role of the right temporo-parietal junction in maintaining a coherent sense of one's body. Neuropsychologia 46:3014–3018.

van den Berg AV, Collewijn H (1988) Directional asymmetries of human optokinetic nystagmus. Exp Brain Res 70:597–604.

Vinken M (2022) Hepatology in space: Effects of spaceflight and simulated microgravity on the liver. Liver Int 42:2599–2606. https://doi.org/10.1111/liv.15444.

Von Holst E, Mittelstaedt H (1950) Das Reafferenzprinzip (Wechselwirkungen zwischen Zentralnervensystem und Peripherie). Naturwissenschaften 37:464–476.

Wade NJ (1973) The effect of water immersion on perception of the visual vertical. Br J Psychol 64:351–361. https://doi.org/10.1111/j.2044-8295.1973.tb01360.x.

Wang L, Liu J, Fan Q, et al. (2021a) Benign paroxysmal positional vertigo as a complication of 90-day head-down bed rest. Eur Arch Otorhinolaryngol 278:683–688. https://doi.org/10.1007/s00405-020-06124-2.

Wang Y, Du B, Wei Y, So RHY (2021b) Visually induced roll circular vection: Do effects of stimulation velocity differ for supine and upright participants? Front Virtual Real 2:1–10. https://doi.org/10.3389/frvir.2021.611214.

Wann JP, Swapp DK (2000) Why you should look where you are going. Nat Neurosci 3:647–648.

Warren WH, Hannon DJ (1990) Eye-movements and optical-flow. J Opt Soc Am Ser A 7:160–169.

Warren WH, Li LY, Ehrlich SM, et al. (1996) Perception of heading during eye-movements uses both optic flow and eye position information. Invest Ophthalmol Vis Sci 37:2066.

Warren PA, Rushton SK (2007) Perception of object trajectory: Parsing retinal motion into self and object movement components. J Vis 7:1–11. https://doi.org/10.1167/7.11.2.

Warren PA, Rushton SK (2008) Evidence for flow-parsing in radial flow displays. Vision Res 48:655–663. https://doi.org/10.1016/j.visres.2007.10.023.

Weisswange TH, Rothkopf CA, Rodemann T, Triesch J (2011) Bayesian cue integration as a developmental outcome of reward mediated learning. PlOS One 6:1–11. https://doi.org/10.1371/journal.pone.0021575.

Wetzig J, Reiser M, Martin E, et al. (1990) Unilateral centrifugation of the otoliths as a new method to determine bilateral asymmetries of the otolith apparatus in man. Acta Astronaut 21:519–525. https://doi.org/10.1016/0094-5765(90)90070-2.

Wilson JA, Anstis SM (1969) Visual delay as a function of luminance. Am J Psychol 82:350–358.

Wilson VJ, Melvill Jones G (1979) Mammalian Vestibular Physiology. Plenum, New York.

Wu Y, Chen K, Ye Y, et al. (2020) Humans navigate with stereo olfaction. Proc Natl Acad Sci U S A 117:16065–16071. https://doi.org/10.1073/pnas.2004642117.

Xu, J., Cui, J., Hao, Y., Xu, B. (2024) Multi-cue guided semi-supervised learning toward target speaker separation in real environments. IEEEACM Trans Audio Speech Lang Proc 32:151–163.

Yardley L (1990) Contribution of somatosensory information to perception of the visual vertical with body tilt and rotating visual-field. Percept Psychophys 48:131–134.

Young MJ, Landy MS, Maloney LT (1993) A perturbation analysis of depth perception from combinations of texture and motion cues. Vision Res 33:2685–2696. https://doi.org/10.1016/0042-6989(93)90228-O.

Young LR, Oman CM, Watt DGD, et al. (1984) Spatial orientation in weightlessness and readaptation to earth's gravity. Science 225:205–208.

Zanchi S, Cuturi LF, Sandini G, Gori M (2022) Interindividual differences influence multisensory processing during spatial navigation. J Exp Psychol Hum Percept Perform 48:174–189. https://doi.org/10.1037/xhp0000973.

Cambridge Elements ≡

Perception

James T. Enns
The University of British Columbia

Editor James T. Enns is Professor at the University of British Columbia, where he researches the interaction of perception, attention, emotion, and social factors. He has previously been editor of the *Journal of Experimental Psychology: Human Perception and Performance* and an associate editor at *Psychological Science, Consciousness and Cognition, Attention Perception & Psychophysics*, and *Visual Cognition*.

About the Series

The modern study of human perception includes event perception, bidirectional influences between perception and action, music, language, the integration of the senses, human action observation, and the important roles of emotion, motivation, and social factors. Each Element in the series combines authoritative literature reviews of foundational topics with forward-looking presentations of the recent developments on a given topic.

Cambridge Elements ☰

Perception

Elements in the Series

A full series listing is available at: www.cambridge.org/EPER

Printed in the United States
by Baker & Taylor Publisher Services